STORY THINKING AND THE REAL-WORLD APPLICATIONS OF SCI-FI AND FANTASY WRITING

STORY THINKING AND THE REAL-WORLD APPLICATIONS OF SCI-FI AND FANTASY WRITING

HELEN MARSHALL, KIM WILKINS AND LISA BENNETT

BLOOMSBURY ACADEMIC

LONDON • NEW YORK • OXFORD • NEW DELHI • SYDNEY

BLOOMSBURY ACADEMIC
Bloomsbury Publishing Plc
50 Bedford Square, London WC1B 3DP, UK
1385 Broadway, New York, NY 10018, USA
29 Earlsfort Terrace, Dublin 2, Ireland

BLOOMSBURY, BLOOMSBURY ACADEMIC and the Diana logo are
trademarks of Bloomsbury Publishing Plc

First published in Great Britain 2025

For legal purposes the Acknowledgements on pp. ix–xi constitute an
extension of this copyright page.

Cover design and illustration by Charlotte Willow Retief

A catalogue record for this book is available from the British Library.

Library of Congress Cataloging-in-Publication Data
Names: Marshall, Helen, 1983- author. | Wilkins, Kim, author. |
Bennett, Lisa (Associate Professor), author.
Title: Story thinking and the real-world applications of sci-fi and fantasy writing /
Helen Marshall, Kim Wilkins and Lisa Bennett.
Description: London ; New York : Bloomsbury Academic, 2025. | Includes index.
Identifiers: LCCN 2024022527 (print) | LCCN 2024022528 (ebook) |
ISBN 9781350359260 (paperback) | ISBN 9781350359253 (hardback) |
ISBN 9781350359277 (pdf) | ISBN 9781350359284 (ebook)
Subjects: LCSH: Science fiction–Authorship. | Fantasy fiction–Authorship. | Creation (Literary,
artistic, etc.) | Influence (Literary, artistic, etc.) | Storytelling. | Creative writing.
Classification: LCC PN3377.5.S3 M37 2025 (print) | LCC PN3377.5.S3 (ebook) |
DDC 808.3/8762–dc23/eng/20240611
LC record available at https://lccn.loc.gov/2024022527
LC ebook record available at https://lccn.loc.gov/2024022528

ISBN: HB: 978-1-3503-5925-3
          PB: 978-1-3503-5926-0
          ePDF: 978-1-3503-5927-7
          eBook: 978-1-3503-5928-4

Typeset by Integra Software Services Pvt. Ltd.
Printed and bound in Great Britain

To find out more about our authors and books visit www.bloomsbury.com
and sign up for our newsletters.

For our children:
Davey, Sigrun, Astrid and Luka.

CONTENTS

ABOUT THE AUTHORS

Helen Marshall is an Associate Professor of Creative Writing at the University of Queensland, Australia. She researches genre fiction, modern and medieval publishing cultures, worldbuilding, franchise writing and the application of creative arts methodologies for interdisciplinary and transdisciplinary ideation. She has won the World Fantasy Award, the British Fantasy Award and the Shirley Jackson Award and her debut novel *The Migration* was one of *The Guardian*'s top science fiction books of the year.

Kim Wilkins is a Professor of Writing at the University of Queensland, Australia. She is a recognized expert on creative practice, genre fiction and the publishing industry. She is the author of more than thirty full-length works of fiction and her work is translated into more than twenty languages globally. Her scholarly research centres on creative communities, such as writing groups and fan cultures. She is most recently the author of *Genre Worlds: Popular Fiction and 21st-Century Book Culture* (2022, with Beth Driscoll and Lisa Fletcher).

Lisa Bennett is an Associate Professor, Creative Writing at Flinders University, Australia, where she researches Viking Age literature, genre fiction and popular culture. Her speculative fiction has won four Aurealis Awards, an Australian National Science Fiction Award and has been nominated for the World Fantasy Award. She facilitates fantasy and horror fiction workshops for Writers SA, regularly reviews for the *ABR* and is a recurrent guest on ABC Radio's 'Book of the Week' segment. With Kim Wilkins, she is the author of *Writing Bestsellers: Love, Money, and Creative Practice* (2021).

ACKNOWLEDGEMENTS

We acknowledge the Traditional Owners and their custodianship of the lands on which this research was conducted, the Turrbal and Jagera people in Brisbane and the Arrernte, Dagoman, First Nations of the South East, First Peoples of the River Murray and Mallee region, Jawoyn, Kaurna, Larrakia, Ngadjuri, Ngarrindjeri, Ramindjeri, Warumungu, Wardaman and Yolngu people in Adelaide. We pay our respects to their Ancestors and their descendants, who continue cultural and spiritual connections to Country. We recognize their valuable contributions to Australian and global society, celebrating the unique knowledges, cultures, histories and languages that have been shared and created for at least 65,000 years.

This scholarly adventure required us to find many allies as we sought to overcome challenges, great and small. We have many to thank.

We begin with Lucy Brown, Senior Commissioning Editor for Literary Studies and Creative Writing, for her faith and encouragement as well as the peer reviewers of our manuscript and Dr Aanchal Vij who helped make the book real.

This work would not have been possible without opportunities afforded us by a range of agencies and organizations. The Defence Science and Technology Group provided a generous grant which supported interviews with writers and the development of one of our first workshop models, and we offer particular thanks to Dr Ksenia Ivanova for her wisdom and enthusiasm.

The Commonwealth Department of Defence also provided support for the Defence Innovation Bridge overseen by Cameron Turner from the University of Queensland Business School. The UNHCR, the UN Refugee Agency, partnered with us, via the Digital Cultures & Societies Hub, to host a scenario lab. The CSIRO Sustainable Futures platform worked with us on a Story Lab devoted to environmental futures in regional Australia. CERN Ideas Square provided valuable opportunities to share ideas with like-minded researchers and practitioners. The ANU Futures Hub has contributed an important community of practice to expand and refine our thinking and meet new collaborators.

The support from our own universities, the University of Queensland and Flinders University, has been important for developing and extending our work. The University of Queensland's Digital Cultures & Societies Hub funded the development of new methodologies and the Faculty of Humanities, Arts and Social Sciences helped us run four workshops with institutions in America, Canada and the United Kingdom to spark the early stages of our thinking. Dr Madonna Devaney, Associate Director, Major Initiatives, of the University of Queensland's Research and Innovation Office has been a staunch champion. We extend our thanks also to Flinders College of Humanities and Social Sciences (especially Professor Sharyn Roach Anleu, Dean of Research, and Narmon Tulsi for support with grant applications). Grateful thanks to our highly valued research assistants Joanne Anderton, Pierce Wilcox and Meg Vann who provided important research support. Further thanks to Associate Professor Stephen Viller, Dr Skye Doherty, Associate Professor Seb Kaempf and Dr Leah Henrickson who have all helped to test and develop our activities. Kathleen Jennings deserves special mention for her sketches, her stories and her wonderful ideas. Further thanks also to our respective research institutions, for their allocation of resources and for opportunities to present research internally during a period of great challenge. Good conversations feed good ideas.

Some of the ideas within this book were developed for journals and we thank the editors and peer reviewers: *Futures*, *The Journal of Futures Studies*, *The Journal of Possibilities Studies* and *TEXT*.

We acknowledge the support, love and patience of our partners and families – you inspire us every day to contribute to building a better world.

Finally, this book would not have been possible without the collective support, expertise and commitment of each individual and organization mentioned above as well as the participants in our interviews, our Labs and workshops. Your fellowship has mattered immensely to us: your curiosity, wisdom, generosity and shared commitment to exploration.

Introduction: Thinking in stories

An invitation to adventure

It is late and you are weary. Come in, shut out the damp chill. The fire is warm and the mead is strong. Don't be alarmed. The whispers aren't true. This isn't a dangerous place, we are not dangerous people, and nor is there dangerous magic in the ceiling beams above you. Settle in. Stretch your legs. Relax for now, because tomorrow you must venture forth to save the world. Do you not remember agreeing to do so?

Don't we all have a responsibility to save the world? In a present that increasingly resembles the dystopian futures imagined by science fiction writers, solutions to complex problems are the first order of business for researchers and thinkers. It would be pleasantly easy if solving them was as simple as taking a quest from a trio of witches in a medieval drinkhouse. Collect six wolf hides, find the secret amulet, poison the ogre under cover of darkness, then battle his kin for the throne. Far more straightforward than, say, stopping the rise of right-wing disinformation while the polar caps melt.

No wonder you are weary.

Solving complex problems isn't entirely dissimilar to a fantasy quest within a particular kind of story. It's easier if you understand the fellowship of heroes journeying with you: the people who have different skills and their motivations for using them. Likewise, this work is undertaken one step at a time, finding the right knowledge and resources and deploying them in different situations, learning from failure until you finally achieve your goal. And it is alert to the environment, responsive to both risks and opportunities. Yet even if you believe solving a complex problem is *nothing at all* like a fantasy quest, then we hope the logic of this kind of speculative storytelling may still provide a fresh perspective, a way of energizing your efforts through language and affinity, and a set of tools for thinking about the future. 'Tell your story', has become a common exhortation – to communicate the value of your research, to sell yourself and your ideas, to get jobs and promotions. But our approach sees stories as more than just structures for communication and persuasion. They are also tools for imagining possibility, predicting chains of causation, connecting people and ideas.

Don't just tell your story, *think* it.

This book outlines an original conceptual model called Story Thinking, which aims to help people think better together and have fun while doing so.

Our cast of characters

But who are we to talk about stories, traveller? Many soothsayers have promised you secret knowledge, haven't they? Before we outline how our advice is different from theirs, let's take a moment to introduce the characters writing this book. The three of us are researchers who are professional science fiction and fantasy (SFF) storytellers, with many books, articles, and stories published between us. But we should drill down beyond the merely descriptive. A good story outlines character motivation to pique readers' interest and allow them to imagine or predict what the characters might do. While it may seem unorthodox to introduce ourselves as characters in an academic book, this introduction shares the logic of a positionality statement. Positionality, a concept in social science, is about acknowledging that research – despite the persistent veneer of objectivity – is actually created by sociomaterially embedded people whose 'lived experience … shape[s] our understanding of the world and the knowledge we produce' (Qin 2016). Understanding those social and material contextual facts about us helps explain why we do what we do and think the way we think.

When Helen finished her PhD in medieval studies, one of her supervisors described her as a cross between a 'hot air balloonist and a truffle pig': someone drawn to the horizon who is also comfortable getting into the messy details. Her academic career has since zigzagged across disciplines and approaches as she seeks to find a balance between the big picture and the facts on the ground. In her creative practice she is naturally drawn to fantasy short stories because they are beautifully crafted imaginative worlds that can be exploded without consequence. She has spent much of her life playing games and make-believe: Dungeons & Dragons, tabletop wargaming, Cthulhu-inspired Live Action Role-Playing, medieval re-enactment. These too are beautifully crafted imaginative worlds that explore systems and new ways of being. Her greatest claim to fame as a writer (besides her World Fantasy Award) is that her debut novel *The Migration* explored a near-future pandemic and was released in 2019, six months before the first coronavirus lockdown. Attracted to shiny objects, Helen is chaotic good and always rolls a thief.

For as long as she can remember, Lisa has been fascinated by things that took place hundreds and hundreds of years ago, things that might possibly happen hundreds and hundreds of years in the future, and things that can only ever happen in magical lands far, far away – but which she *really* wishes could be real. (When told to 'live in the moment', nobody ever specifies that the moment has to be *now*. In Lisa's opinion, *now* is so much less interesting than *once upon a time*.) Driven by her love of illustration and medieval fantasy, she undertook a Bachelor of Fine Arts in Canada, mistakenly thinking that a degree in contemporary abstract painting and weird photography would somehow lead her into a career as a graphic designer. All along, what really drove her was a deep-seated love of reading and storytelling. So, while undertaking her PhD in medieval Icelandic literature, she finally started writing her own strange and wondrous stories and hasn't stopped since. Lisa is neutral good and always rolls an elf sorcerer.

Kim often tells people that when she was born she had the full complement of human emotions plus one extra called 'story'. Alongside love, anger, joy and so on, she can recognize and feel 'story' in her body as both an anticipatory thrill as ideas join to other ideas in satisfying chains, and as a sweet little clunk in her chest, when a plot idea that has been set up earlier circles back and becomes meaningful. In chasing those feelings, which are very dear to her, she has written dozens of novels: the novel form suits her intellectual craving for complex plotting as well as her serial obsessions with various historical periods and settings, where she likes to set up camp in her imagination for long stays. Kim is chaotic neutral and always rolls a barbarian.

Enough about us for now. We aren't the only characters in this book. You are in here too. Perhaps you are an entrepreneur or designer who seeks greater engagement with your collaborators or those impacted by the products you are developing. Perhaps you are a research scientist or systems thinker working doggedly on a small part of a large problem, hoping to connect to others. Perhaps you are a facilitator who has been charged with helping a dysfunctional team collaborate better so they can work on organizational solutions. Perhaps you are simply curious. This book is intended for all of you and many others, with the caveat that our methods have particular usefulness for teams. While Story Thinking could be adapted and applied more broadly for individual personal development, this book is designed to get people working together quickly on imagining solutions to complex, and often interdisciplinary, problems.

What is a story?

There are words that have been so overused that, like a stone tumbled too long by the sea, they have worn smooth. 'Story' is one such word where critical traction has become almost impossible. It might be useful to start with what researchers have written about what stories *do*. Brian Boyd's 2009 *On the Origin of Stories: Evolution, Cognition, and Fiction* argues that our stories are an evolutionary adaptation key to our survival as a species. Jonathan Gottschall's 2012 *The Storytelling Animal: How Stories Make Us Human* suggests that stories are a kind of social glue and allow us to practise situations imaginatively before we enter them. Lisa Cron's 2012 *Wired for Story* focuses on the brain chemistry of story and how anticipation engages our imaginations. Will Storr's 2020 *The Science of Storytelling* approaches stories from a psychological perspective, arguing that they prime our brains to make sense of change and the unexpected. Sarah Dillon and Clare Craig's 2022 *Storylistening: Narrative Evidence and Public Reasoning* holds that stories shape the way that the public imagines and understands events and identities, including their own.

As for what stories *are*, we could turn to the *Oxford Dictionary of English*, which defines a story as 'an account of imaginary or real people and events told for entertainment' or 'an account of past events in someone's life or in the development of something'. Its etymology derives via Middle English, a shortening of the Anglo-Norman *estorie* from Latin *historia*, meaning 'a historical account or representation' (*Oxford Dictionary of English* 2023). It appears story has always been a tool that connects reality and imagination. As the books listed above indicate, stories may be imaginary but they always connect to real physiological, social and evolutionary effects.

Our definition, for the purpose of this book and derived from our practice, is that a story is an account of something happening to someone (individually or as a group) somewhere, but also, importantly, it is an account of that someone's *relationship* with that something and somewhere; that is, it always has a dimension related to feeling and reaction. Beyond that basic definition, there are countless possibilities for plot structures, character actions and craft-driven complexions. We will touch on some of these throughout, but at its base: something happens to someone somewhere and they react and have feelings about it. Importantly, even if the story is based on imaginary events and imaginary people, it exists in the real world and invites people to reflect on its contents. A story, then, is a real-world model for understanding how (often imaginary) people relate to their problems. And aren't we all people with problems?

A key distinction we want to make up front is the one between story and plot. We have a whole chapter on plot (see Chapter 2). These chains of cause and effect are often called 'stories' but the two words, in our view, are nowhere near interchangeable. A good metaphor might be to think about plot as the spine or skeleton of a story, giving it shape and form, but a skeleton alone does not make a full body. As Christopher Priest told us in an interview:

> Plot and story are connected, but they are not the same thing, and they are not the only thing that matters. Think of them as a core, an armature. Wind around them thinly, and you end up with second-rate genre writing: someone getting in a spaceship to go somewhere to do something. An intelligent reader demands and expects more – a good writer will have the same expectations. Wind it more thickly. So we enter the world of location, character, mood, place, motive, emotion, romance, language. These are not necessary ingredients. They are the result of holistic imagining.
>
> (2022)

While Priest's assumptions about what readers and writers might demand or expect are readily problematizable (there are plenty of intelligent people who would delight in simply imagining a spaceship going somewhere to do something), the point here is 'holistic imagining'. A skeleton is not a body.

But much like a body without a skeleton, without a plot the story is an unpleasant mess.

Luckily for you, dear reader, we have written many stories and taught creative writing to many students. Our definition of story revolves around four elements: character (someone), conflict (something), context (somewhere) and makes room for the fundamental importance of style.

Character is about who the story belongs to, whose thoughts and feelings we'll have access to, what their stake in the story is, and, importantly how their backstory and personality will influence the choices they make and the reactions that they have. A character is a human access point into a story: they experience it for us and make it meaningful. The character provides the emotional ups and downs, the vertical movement of the story. The character must feel real to us, real enough that we can empathize and relate even if they are doing and feeling things that we would never do ourselves. The character makes the events concrete, not abstract.

However, there is no story without *conflict*. You can do all your best work creating a character with backstory and quirks and flaws and Dickensian catchphrases, but until you give them a problem, you don't have a story. A story describes the relationship between a character and a conflict (or people and a problem, as we wrote above). When the character has a problem, they try to solve it. The steps they take, the setbacks they endure, all go towards making up the plot, the horizontal movement of the story. The distinction of plot driven versus character driven is nonsense. A story cannot afford to ever lose track of either. The character moves the plot and is moved by the plot; the plot moves the character and is moved by the character. The trick in managing plot is your ability to be able to imagine and calibrate multiple possible outcomes and choose one that is both plausible and interesting. That might mean that sometimes conflict has to come from the flanks to throw the character into chaos.

Context encompasses setting but is so much more than just the usual things we associate with setting: time and place. Context is not a backdrop, against which characters and conflicts work themselves out. Context is embedded history, lore, rules, logic, culture, norms and so on. SFF writers call this worldbuilding because that's what it is: creating a whole world, inside which the story takes place. Importantly, every context provides limitations and affordances for the character and conflict. The context can change the complexion of everything. The context captures and contains the horizontal and vertical movement, giving it the multidimensional quality we recognize in great stories.

The final, but also indispensable, element of storytelling is, of course, *style*: the choice of words and images and conventions we use to invite the reader into our story and make them stay. This in no way has to mean a platonic ideal of literary value. If you're a lover of space opera and see the words 'pod bay doors', it doesn't matter how many times you have read about pod bay doors. They mean something special to you, and you will happily read about them again. The words, the language, the imagery, even the tropes storytellers use do matter. They engage the reader and bring them into the story, and they can even bond the reader with other readers through shared investments in certain types of language and ideas.

What is Story Thinking?

Our model of Story Thinking, then, elevates these four aspects of craft to ways of thinking about problems. Setting becomes 'inhabit'. Creating and inhabiting a storyworld is a valuable tool to situate a problem in its context and explore limits and affordances in an imaginative space or speculative environment. Plotting becomes 'envision'. We use cause and effect to extrapolate from different divergence points and speculate on multiple outcomes. SFF specializes in defamiliarization, pushing away from probability to work in the space of possibility, where we generate new ideas and scenarios and look for the shadows of the unexpected and the orthogonal. Characterization becomes 'empathize'. Being able to imagine the experience of others, especially others radically different from ourselves, is key both to telling stories and codesigning solutions for complex problems. We offer tools for perspective taking, developing empathy and imagining people with disparate and surprising backgrounds, histories and experiences, especially those who are often overlooked. And style becomes 'engage': the key to the kind of invitation and communication that bring people together into a Story Thinking experience, and make it enjoyable and memorable.

Why think in stories?

In our introductions, we all earnestly gestured towards our love of thinking in stories. We became creative writers because stories – whether reading them, watching them, writing them, or playing them – meant something to us. Over the years, as audiences and then amateurs and then finally as professionals, we came to understand the craft of storytelling implicitly and tacitly. As academics, we were then asked to explicate that knowledge and formalize it into transferable and digestible lessons: how to create a character, how to generate possibilities in plot and so on.

But in other ways, our knowledge of story affected our lives. We were complimented for our ability to see a range of people's perspectives, or we were able to generate weird and engaging answers to old questions easily, or we found strategy alarmingly easy because in many ways it was just like plotting: stand at this node *here* and choose a direction that will bear fruit. And often we were told our success in such endeavours was down to our being 'creative' (see Chapter 6 for a stern talking-to about dividing people into creative and non-creative). In fact, this range of enhanced or even just nuanced abilities was due to our familiarity with stories: those little models of people and their problems.

Creative writing has a ready set of skills for developing the open-ended thinking needed in solving complex problems: including the ability to tolerate ambiguity; perspective taking; negotiation and integration of conflicting or contradictory systems; and finding useful metaphors and shared language to transcend disciplinary divides (Bracken and Oughton 2006; Repko and Szostack 2011; Gibson, Crea and Chambers 2018; Hardy 2018; Gilligan 2019). For us, though, this kind of thinking (which Helen dubbed Story Thinking in the middle of the pandemic in 2020), has never been separable from our attachments to the genre of speculative fiction, also known as science fiction and fantasy, also known as SFF. While most writers across all genres may have expert knowledge of characterization and developing detailed settings, SFF emphasizes other significant elements, including the creation of new or imaginative worlds with diverse inhabitants; a focus on large-scale conflicts arising from cause-and-effect chains; a set of familiar and widely known tropes; and, crucially, an expectation of departure from the 'known', which make it particularly appropriate for this kind of work.

SFF has a long association with scientific advancement, most notably the space race. Milburn (2008) explores how the development of nanotechnologies and the visions for its future uses are inextricably linked to science fiction. Likewise, Kirby (2010) discusses how cinematic representations of possible technologies can inspire researchers. Vertisi's sociological study of NASA (2019) demonstrates the impact of *Star Trek* and other science fiction classics to motivate individuals, and Vint (2021) more broadly studies the role of science fiction in directing fields such as artificial intelligence, genomic research and biomedicine. Defence experts Ryan and Finney have written about the value of SFF in 'inspir[ing] divergent thinking about advanced technologies and how to apply them in concert with new ideas and new organizations' (2018). More widely, SFF has found useful overlaps with design prototyping (Johnson 2011) and ideation (Kotecha et al. 2021), public policy (Belton and Dillon 2021) and futures literacy (Liveley, Slocombe and Spiers 2021). It's important to note that while these examples show the impact of science fiction on technological development, they tend to address the consumption rather than the production of stories. The potential of thinking like an SFF writer is amplified by creating rather than just reading or viewing: Story Thinkers understand the problems from the inside, rather than analysing them from the outside.

More than this, we argue that to think in stories is to think creatively in a way intended not just to develop novel results but also useful ones. Here we find support in research into creative training by Fletcher and Benveniste (2022) who argue that narrative cognition can be more powerful than divergent thinking in navigating uncertain problem spaces. Like us, they identify important features of narrative cognition that align to what we would consider to be elements of craft: worldbuilding techniques (aligned with our domain Inhabit), action-generating techniques (aligned with our domain Envision) and perspective-taking techniques (aligned with our domain Empathize). Yet as practitioners we recognize that undergirding our domains is a practised pattern for how we as writers imagine. That is, we move back and forth fluidly from invention (putting new ideas into play), extrapolation (extending trends, patterns or relationships to fill in gaps) and calibration (determining fitness for purpose).

An example can help flesh out how this skill set works in practice. Whenever we embark upon creating imaginary worlds, either singly or collaboratively, we find a starting point, often a 'What if?' question that provokes our curiosity. As we make a first foray into answering the question, we begin to think more deeply. One detail tends to lead naturally to the next. We ask ourselves questions as they occur to us and search for answers that resonate or align with what we have already decided. Often this mimics the pattern of a game from improvisational theatre called, 'Yes, and … ' in which one actor makes a statement and their partner immediately replies, 'Yes, and … ', accepting what has been said and building on it without ever creating a contradiction. Imagine the following series of exchanges and you will get the gist:

'What if I set my story in Australia in 2040?'

'Yes, and in that world, climate change is forcing people to relocate from
    coastal areas and floodplains … '

'Yes, and so the cost of real estate begins to shoot up … '

'Yes, and the government is forced to buy up the inhabitable land … '

'Yes, and they risk going bankrupt so they sell portions off to China … '

The first question, 'What if?' sets up the basic premise of the storyworld by putting a new idea into play. Each of the following exchanges accepts the premise and asks, 'What else?' and by doing so extrapolates new possibilities while closing down others. A basic thread of logic links the suggestions, becoming more powerful as the game continues. Of course, at any stage of this game, a critical partner could say, 'Yes, but what if it's New Zealand they sell the land to?' or 'Instead, what about … '. This is how creative writers test and calibrate their ideas: sometimes checking for plausibility or consistency with what has come before, sometimes probing whether the direction of travel is likely to generate useful results.

We can see an example of how this works in how author Naomi Alderman talks about writing her 2016 novel *The Power*, which explores a hypothetical version of the present in which adolescent females become endowed with the ability to release electricity from their fingertips. With this quirk of genetic mutation, the world undergoes a profound transformation as women gain an indisputable physical advantage and gender hierarchies are ultimately flipped. Alderman describes her creative process with this creative pattern of thinking. She began by asking herself,

> *[w]hat if* women and not men were the sex who could do more physical harm, who could cause more pain? Do we think that, in those circumstances, women would remain peaceful and loving and kind and lovely, or do we not?
>
> And let's have a think about *how those situations would play out*. And I really went into the book thinking, I want to know, too. I want to know *what*

would happen in these circumstances, and then just *following the logic* of the characters and the plot through to work out what I thought the answer was.

(PBS NewsHour, 2019, emphasis our own)

Throughout this book we shorthand this pattern of inventing new ideas, extrapolating possibilities and calibrating the results to three simple questions: What if? What else? What for? As you will see, these aren't limited only to the creation of new worlds but repeat across all our four domains. We build up a sense of characters by choosing initial traits and using them to slowly increase complexity and psychological depth. We create plots by beginning with an inciting event that sparks the action and then we determine what consequences may follow. Invention gets us started with the kernel of an idea, extrapolation allows us to develop that idea, and calibration is the gut check that keeps us on the rails, where we apply critical thinking and ask ourselves, 'Have we made the right choices? Are they leading us in the right direction? What do we want to accomplish with this?' Our fourth domain, which aligns with style, neglected by Fletcher and Benveniste (and indeed many others), is that the pattern of possibility generation, progression and testing is fundamentally bound by language. While we would encourage all researchers to practise these skills regularly, what this book aims to do is to show some of the tried and tested strategies that can help people without fifty-four combined years of practitioner experience learn to use these skills quickly and enjoyably.

Story Thinking and other kinds of thinking

Design thinking

We aren't the first people to use the word 'thinking' as a suffix on a conceptual model for problem solving. In early innovation curricula we see 'creative thinking', 'visual thinking' and 'ambidextrous thinking' emphasized, all 'mindset changes that aid creativity' (von Thienen et al. 2018). A popular approach to this sort of work in recent years is design thinking, which draws on the expertise of design practitioners who prototype new products or services to find commercial solutions to real-world problems. Design thinking is a problem-solving approach that emphasizes empathy, creativity and iteration to develop innovative solutions. It involves understanding user needs, generating potential solutions, and prototyping and testing ideas to arrive at user-centred designs. The consulting firm IDEO has been particularly successful in promoting a version of this: human-centred design. Their toolkit presents creative exercises that help commercial organizations imagine the needs and contexts of their products' users (Kelley 2005; Brown 2008). We draw parallels with this work because it's accessible to a wide audience, it has achieved good results and it requires relatively little infrastructure. Story Thinking complements design thinking and indeed our strategies and exercises could easily be used to augment elements of design approaches such as the use of personas, which we discuss in Chapter 3. But fundamentally, Story Thinking has different strengths.

Because design thinking emerges from principles used to solve engineering problems, it tends to place more weight on creating and testing solutions. Rittel (1988) finds many proponents of design thinking divide their process into two distinct phases: identifying and formulating the problem, and structuring the solution. Dinar et al. (2011) argue that good designers ought to spend more time on finding ways to produce flexible and dynamic problem representations. Ho (2001) states that expert designers decompose a problem (break it into manageable sub-problems), decide on a final goal, work backward to determine what is needed and then work forward again to find the solution. This mirrors our own experience with design approaches: the most successful are those that spend time understanding the problem, before structuring a solution and beginning a robust phase of testing. Yet we have also found, either as a result of the disciplinary underpinnings of design or because of poor practice (or perhaps both), that many applications of design thinking move as quickly as possible to the solution pathway. This orientation moves emphasis away from problem definition, arguably the most important part of a design process, to mobilizing an outcome (often one that can be brought quickly to market). Leifer and Meinel (2018: 1) call this 'solution fixation'. In particular, borrowing from the work of Kees Dorst, they show five types of design thinking most likely to fall into this solution fixation trap: the 'lone warrior' who wants to own the solution; 'freeze the world' which wants to ignore change and use 'static thinking'; the 'self-made box' which demands we solve future solutions the way we have solved them in the past; 'rational high ground' which asserts rationality and practicality over creativity and possibility; and 'identification' where both problem and solution are framed in ways the organization has always used to frame them and can easily continue to frame them, or what Leifer and Meinel call 'organizational autopoiesis' (ibid.: 3). While all of these ways of thinking are examples of fixed mindset or closed thinking, Leifer and Meinel argue that 'analytical and generative attention' are better directed to a problem-oriented mindset that is more open-ended (ibid.: 3).

By contrast, Story Thinking is fundamentally not solution-driven: that isn't to say Story Thinkers are not interested in solutions (we are) but that we are more interested in creating new understandings of the problem itself and its permutations, while recognizing that the work of providing the solutions will belong to others. What does this mean in practice? According to our Story Thinking model, we would note that the solution-oriented design approaches tend to be very focused on deciding on then testing a critical pathway (which we would align with plotting, see Chapter 2), but they neglect the other aspects of story: characters with their backstories and motivations; the setting they find themselves in; and the language necessary to keep solutions open to imaginative, figurative and collaborative thinking.

Story Thinking, with its focus on the model of people and their problems, may also be more agile in understanding how a particular solution pathway might need to be adjusted or indeed abandoned as its contexts change. Once we introduce the extreme contingency of a model with multiple facets that generate multiple possibilities, we are forced to explore a problem space from multiple angles, dipping in and out of phases of ideation and solution generation. This, then, is another of Story Thinking's great strengths: it aims to produce insights that can help navigate complexity, rather than fragile solutions that are easily disrupted.

Systems thinking

Systems thinking is another way of understanding problems that allows room for complexity. Michael C. Jackson traces the origins of systems thinking across disciplines, including philosophy, science and social science. The coherent concept of systems thinking arose in the second half of the twentieth century, driven by systems engineering, as the field of engineering 'began to extend its scope from individual components to the design of complex systems' (2019: 177). Jackson suggests it has now become its own 'transdiscipline' (ibid.: xxv). Bearing this out, Adams elaborates a methodology called 'system of systems engineering' (or SoSE) (2011) as a way to apply systems thinking, outlining a series of principles for thinking through complexity, which is highly complex in itself. Systems thinking, then, is a 'study of wholes, and their emergent properties ... put on an equal footing with the study of parts' (Jackson 2019: xix). It's easy to understand why a holistic perspective that sees how the various parts interrelate is an appealing way to bring researchers from disparate disciplines and backgrounds together for an 'integrated understanding of the problem and integrated suggestions for dealing with the problem' (Pohl and Hadorn 2008: 13).

As Adams's research shows, systems thinking is itself a discipline with a specific language derived from engineering, which does not necessarily lead to 'transparent expression' (Masini 2014). For example, the International Council on Systems Engineering (INCOSE) has made attempts to standardize systems thinking, including proposing key engineering terminology such as maturity models, process dimensions, quality attributes and information items. Such technical terms may prove a barrier to engagement. Barry Richmond, a leader in the field of systems thinking, writes: 'As interdependency increases … [i]t's not good enough simply to get smarter and smarter about our particular "piece of the rock." We must have a common language and framework for sharing our specialized knowledge, expertise and experience with "local experts" from other parts of the web. We need a systems Esperanto' (1991: 3). The language of storytelling, e.g. words like plot, character and setting, or the vocabulary of science fiction and fantasy, widely known from SFF across media, are a little more straightforward to grasp. Story Thinking then offers a common language for situating, mapping and un-siloing specialized knowledge, which gets disparate researchers and stakeholders in the same problem space and working quickly and collaboratively on building solutions.

As well as offering a ready language for systems thinking, Story Thinking can add dimension to a systems view of a problem. Systems mapping may represent all of the *things* in a system, organized by various principles of hierarchy, emergence, communications and control (Adams 2011: 122–4) and may indeed be able to find connections between these things and judge potential risks and benefits at these nodes, according to the SoSE framework of principles. However, the number of possibilities generated at these nodes can be multiplied by considering the environments in which the encounters take place (setting) or the people who interact with them (character). For example, a map of military technology like the one devised by Ivanova, Elsawah and Fidock and based on SoSE principles (2020: 429) shows how personal monitoring devices and communications networks in a system may interact, and predicts from there some risks and benefits. But imagining how those outcomes are changed if the tech is used by a young soldier who has grown up in a liberal democracy versus a bad actor who has grown up under an authoritarian regime, allows further nuance and possibility. This dimension is, of course, proliferative, demonstrating how Story Thinking tends towards open-endedness and problem exploration.

We have written several times already of stories as models for understanding people and problems; we hold that they are systems themselves, and so dropping a problem into the model of a story allows for a different kind of imaginative analysis. This book outlines the ways that analysis might happen.

Futures thinking

Futures thinking, or futures studies as we call it elsewhere in this book, has obvious overlaps with Story Thinking. One particular area of shared interest is scenario planning, which is in itself a kind of storytelling (though one we find tends to be more strictly related to the narration of a certain place and time, with less attention to other dimensions). Scenario planning originated in the Cold War, when the threat of nuclear conflict challenged American strategists to plan for situations of mutually assured destruction without precedent. Herman Kahn and colleagues at the Rand Corporation pioneered the approach of using imagined futures as 'strange aids to thought' (Scoblic 2020). It has since remained an ongoing practice in Defence. Research by Matt Carr maps contemporary military futurist activities from the 1997 Global Trends Report of the US National Intelligence Council through the rise of wargaming to the crisis of 9/11, which he sees almost as a genre in and of itself, owing 'as much to apocalyptic Hollywood movies as it does to the cold war tradition of "scenario planning"' (2010: 13). Throughout this period, as Carr argues, it was also adopted within the corporate sphere. In the early 1970s, Shell experimented with scenarios described as 'a potentially better framework for thinking about the future than forecasts' (Wack 1985). The alternative futures presented by Wack's team ultimately positioned Shell to navigate the shocks that ensued following the Six Day War and the subsequent oil embargo by the Organization of the Petroleum Exporting Countries (OPEC).

Within this context, Jenny Andersson provides fascinating insights to science fiction authors' engagement with futurism – including Clarke, Asimov, Lem and Marcuse – to demonstrate 'the struggle against the bomb from the late 1950s included the idea that the armament process was determined by a set of technological and scientific logics that could only be broken through the imagination' (2018: 159–60). Recent Humanities scholars and arts practitioners have built up the links between science fiction and imagining the future, sometimes within military or corporate environments, but just as often aligning with other areas such as innovation which are less obviously linked to risk mitigation, expanding the tools and purposes which underlie futures work. Liveley, Slocombe and Spiers use oral storytelling, improvisation and collaborative theatre to create an anticipatory future practice, arguing the skills and competencies of literary criticism can 'expose the mechanisms and heuristics which we draw upon in making sense of the possible worlds that the future represents' (2021: 4). Finn and Wylie (2021: 2) outline an Imaginative Collaborative Framework designed specifically for enhancing collective capacity to imagine in groups. A recent special issue of the journal *Vector* (Walton and Levontin 2023) was devoted specifically to overlaps between science fiction and futures studies.

We see the methodological plurality of futures studies as one of its strengths. While not all our work is rigidly futures focused, certainly *some* of it has been, as our case studies show. What Story Thinking can contribute here is a developed methodology for worldbuilding which foregrounds both the systemic level and the local level; a way of thinking about how to incorporate both incremental changes and tipping points; a focus on characters as driving forces of change or vantage points into a complex system; an attention to the aesthetics of the world, the aesthetics of the 'genre' of scenario planning and the aesthetics of the experience of scenario planning itself. In reading through the contents of this book we expect futurists will find some material that resonates with their practice, some that might augment it and some that might challenge it.

Story Thinking and practice

A name like Story Thinking may have you wondering if all we do is sit and contemplate. Quite the opposite. While Story Thinking is a conceptual model, its chief value comes in *doing*. We mobilize Story Thinking through collaborative, interactive activities, which we call Story Labs. We have included a range of these as case studies at the ends of our chapters to show the kinds of problems Story Thinking can address as well as the specific techniques we have used. In this way, Story Thinking shares some of the logic of practice-based research, which is how we talk about creative writing in the academy. Research that uses a methodology from practice (in this case creative writing) usually leads to an output that is creative. It is sometimes seen as a digression from the hard facts of quantitative research, and a kind of 'liquid knowledge' as artist Marina Abramovic called it, or knowledge that can find its way through a system in flow (Nelson 2013: 52). The premier tool for developing creative outputs in the academy is the workshop, developed at the University of Iowa in the mid-twentieth century, a model of bringing creative ideas into dialogue with others to refine them (Vanderslice 2010: 31). Originally, robust criticism (even cruel criticism) was seen as a way to develop a writer's resilience. While there are still aficionados of this kind of workshopping, contemporary creative writing classrooms, which are often populated by young and very inexperienced writers, are more likely to thrive on collaborative activities that build the writer and the work (ibid.: 32). Gross calls a creative writing workshop 'a very human situation' (2010: 52) and notes that a workshop 'is not a *thing*. The real thing is a group of people, brought together in a time and place' (ibid.: 55), emphasizing the social and material aspects of creative collaboration. The goal of a workshop is human cooperation around research conducted via practice. The logic of the workshop pervades our Story Labs.

However, we have deliberately chosen to use the metaphor of the lab rather than the workshop simply because it describes more accurately what is done when we think in stories together. Rather than working through steps towards a predetermined goal (workshop), we foreground tests, investigations, experiments (laboratory). We also choose not to use the word 'workshop' as it strongly connotes pedagogy. While we are certain Story Thinking as a method for knowledge generation and transfer could be used in classrooms, that is not what it is designed for. We claim no deep knowledge of its value or application in pedagogical settings; for us, Story Thinking is a tool for research, problem definition and solution generation.

Finally, Story Thinking also shares a logic with, although is distinct from, storytelling. What the three authors of this book do as storytellers in practice is in many ways a legacy model of storytelling, though it may be the most commonly understood one: we make up stories for other people to consume. However, increasingly, storytelling is a powerful tool for connection and for exchanging knowledge and has been used across many domains. For example, Silva and Silva coin the term 'collaborative storytelling' to describe a theory of social change based on reflection and communication of the relationship between self and other in organizations (2022: 5). Quesenbery and Coolsen note the predominance of use of the term storytelling in business and marketing, and advocate for its use in gaining attention for brands (2023: 7). Kayılı and Erdel describe a drama-based storytelling model suitable for children, where a narrator invites them to occupy different character positions to improve their problem-solving skills (2021: 45). Alfonso et al. write of the mental health benefits in social work of storytelling, particularly in 'enabling the verbalisation of difficult feelings' (2022: 157). Storytelling centres on the pleasure of story to engage both the teller and the listener (or the writer and the reader, etc.), though the aims of that engagement differ across these disciplines.

Story Thinking also centres on the pleasure of story to engage, but articulates an expanded notion of story's benefits beyond reflection and communication, to a kind of systematic imagining, with the goal of understanding problems more capaciously. Like creative writers in the legacy understanding of storytelling mentioned above, Story Thinkers use the methodology of storytelling to generate detailed models and explore them from multiple perspectives.

A last note on how practice intersects with the aims of this book. We have established our credentials as practising professional writers already and noted that it affects our position in researching and writing about Story Thinking. It is worth adding that the position comes with certain insider knowledge: with the volume of creative writing we have generated between us, we cannot (nor would we want to) pretend to be newbies to the craft. While we don't want to suggest that we know everything about creative writing, we can't hide our extensive knowledge and slavishly cite other writers as though they know more or better. Nor should we need to rely on the citation of a researcher to prove something that we know experientially through practice. We are all writers of international renown. This is not to say that we have jettisoned the idea of academic objectivity and referencing other thinkers all together, as we hope this introduction has already proven. We love making things up, but we wouldn't do that in an academic book. Rather, the research in this book is partly autoethnographic (Adams, Jones and Ellis 2014). Autoethnography is a self-reflective practice that is rooted in our personal experience and which aims to balance 'intellectual rigor and emotional investment' or a kind of critical proximity (Wilkins, Driscoll and Fletcher 2022: 21). We see this as a key strength of our work and an offer of reassurance about the robustness of our critical model.

Ready to begin your Story Thinking adventure?

Although we are all creative writers, we recognize stories are told in many ways and enjoy many forms of storytelling ourselves. Alongside our deep love of the written word, Story Thinking is also an homage to – and our own interpretation of – roleplaying games like Dungeons & Dragons. This is most apparent in the tone, titles and emphasis on creative play in the theories and practices informing this book. Perhaps less apparent, but no less significant, is the palpable sense that Story Thinking is the product of fun, lively and rewarding collaboration between three writer-friends, which channels the spirit of 'awesomeness' inherent in such improvisational games (see Chapter 5). Our aim with this work is to delight and inspire as much as to challenge, question and provoke thought.

The nature of print publication being what it is (a static recording of vibrant ideas rather than an interactive electronic and/or more organic form of communication like texting or talking – along with our ingrained and perpetual investment as creative writers to tell a logical story) has led us to carefully consider (read: agonize over) the structure and order of chapters in this work. Nevertheless, we invite you to stray from the straightforward path of the quest we've laid out, if you're feeling adventurous: grab an eight-sided dice and let the fates guide your experience of this book.

If you roll a one, you'll encounter the first of our four domains: Inhabit. In this chapter, we explore one of the most recognizable aspects of SFF writing: worldbuilding or setting. Before we begin to think about individual characters, their motivations and the plots they drive, we need to consider the physical, environmental and cultural contexts they inhabit. SFF worlds are, in our view, particularly useful for thinking through real-world problems. When they are built effectively, these settings are enchanting and edifying. They are complex systems that impose rules, logic and restrictions upon the beings (human or otherwise) presented within each narrative and thereby determine how their storylines can unfold. By asking us to imagine new and unexpected places, they compel us to think in new and unexpected ways. Worldbuilding can also be a pleasurable and powerful tool for collaboration. It is immersive and outward-looking rather than introspective. In this chapter, we outline specific principles and strategies that SFF writers use to create effective and immersive storyworlds and show how you can use them to think creatively together.

Rolling a two will take you to our second domain: Envision. Here, we investigate the role of conflict in stories: the crises, choices and consequences that shape (and are shaped by) character actions and their settings. We discuss how sequences of problems, and the search for solutions to these problems, can be strung like pearls on a string to create strong and interesting plots. In this chapter, we think about plots not just as fast-paced vehicles that whisk us away from reality for a while but as tools that Story Thinkers can wield for envisioning and reimagining real-world events and their consequences. Drawing on plotting techniques, we show how to develop these storylines from inciting incidents through probable, possible, implausible and even weird pathways, all the way to logical (and often surprising) conclusions.

Roll a three to consider how SFF characters are crafted to make us empathize: with them and, by extension, with real people around us. In our exploration of this domain, we situate characters as narrative focal points through whose observations, behaviours, beliefs and actions readers live and think vicariously. Whether they're human, alien, supernatural or mythical – or something else entirely – well-crafted characters have compelling motivations. They have individual perspectives, personal histories, convictions, tangible goals. They act in credible ways. They may think or do things we've never imagined before, things impossible to think or do in our own world, but they will nevertheless follow a coherent logic that readers can understand. Effective characters bridge gaps in experience and first-hand knowledge: they give us intimate insights into their realities so that we might reflect upon and reconsider our own. In this chapter, we discuss how many approaches to characterization, from archetypal, 'flat' and/or shallow to incredibly detailed and individualistic 'rounded' figures, can help us to understand diverse perspectives and empathize our way into more productive creative collaboration.

When you roll a four, we'll invite you to consider the ways in which words engage the imagination, shape our experiences and influence expectations (both in fiction and in life). Language is a portal to new worlds. It can instantly welcome us in or effectively keep us out. It might be very easy to open or quite difficult to crack but, either way, that door points us in a particular direction: it frames the place we're currently standing and acts as an entry point (or barrier) for understanding the world beyond. In writing, the style of a piece – its tone, narrative voice, use or lack of metaphors and similes, attention to (and experimentation with) grammar and punctuation – fundamentally shape how we read. This chapter explores how style enriches plot, character and setting, and aims to show how expertly wielded words can build connection and understanding within and between diverse groups.

The second part of this book moves beyond a strict consideration of the writer's toolbox to show how our approach can be operationalized within Story Labs for teams working on complex problems. *On your next roll, the die balances on its edge, showing both five and six.* At their core, these two chapters are about fostering creativity, collaboration and strong fellowships. Story Thinking asks us to do something unexpected with the skills we already have, stretching them in more imaginative, creative and communal ways that allow us to be playful and productive. In Chapter 5, we examine specific strategies for building an awesome group dynamic, one built on a foundation of good communication, established boundaries and clear rules, and which encourages participants to take creative risks. Chapter 6 takes these ideas into the realm of James Paul Gee's 'affinity spaces' (2005) and demonstrates how bringing diverse groups of people together can engender a sense of shared purpose and common understanding. We highlight the significance of SFF storytelling and fan culture as touchstones for group-generated metaphors and in-jokes that can bind fellowships together in these situations, as well as flatten hierarchies and emphasize the power of improvisation, fun and play in establishing a sense of belonging that's conducive to creating new knowledge together.

Roll a seven to get the epic loot. Our Dungeon Master's Guide shows how to put into practice everything we've presented in this book. Here, we present sample outlines for Story Labs we have run, a series of creative exercises informed by our four domains and valuable tips and tricks from our own practice that will be powerful potions against wasted time and admin-related headaches. And if you *roll an eight*, you can skip immediately to the final chapter, where we outline some of the aspects of creative and intellectual growth that Story Thinking may offer to you and your teams.

So, what are you waiting for, traveller? The road from here will not grow any easier if you hesitate. But once you begin this journey, you may find new vantage points for viewing the road and its many crooks, dead ends and sudden steep drops. Negotiating a path through difficulty can be achieved in many different ways. The concept and method we present herein should be easily comprehensible and enjoyable at least and inspire new thinking at best.

Welcome to your Story Thinking adventure.

1

Inhabit: Storyworlds and the rules of the game

Introduction

Once upon a time, at the edge of a forest, there lived a poor woodcutter, his wife and his two children, Hansel and Gretel …

Like a spell, these words plunge us into a storyworld, a fairy-tale landscape populated by wolves and witches, kings and queens, tricksters, lost children and giants. Through years of cultural exposure, many of you will know intimately the rules that govern this space: be wary of strangers (but also be kind to strangers because mercy and generosity make one virtuous), do not stray from the path (but also allow yourself to get lost because that is the only way to find riches), work hard (but also find ways to cheat because some tasks are intended to trap you forever).

Now pay attention to the incantation that summons this world to mind. *Once upon a time, at the edge of a forest …* We are given a time that is not really a time and a place that could be anywhere. Contrast this functional haziness with the gorgeous specificity of the opening to Angela Carter's retelling of the classic fairy tale 'The Bloody Chamber':

I remember how, that night, I lay awake in the wagon-lit in a tender, delicious ecstasy of excitement, my burning cheek pressed against the impeccable linen of the pillow and the pounding of my heart mimicking that of the great pistons ceaselessly thrusting the train that bore me through the night, away from Paris, away from girlhood, away from the white, enclosed quietude of my mother's apartment, into the unguessable country of marriage.

([1979] 2006: 1)

This is not a story of anywhere and anywhen. The details here are far more concrete: the 'wagon-lit', the 'impeccable linen of the pillow' and the 'great pistons' of the train surging away from Paris. At least, nominally, the opening of the story locates it in the real world.

Both settings do specific creative work. They anchor their stories, and suggest, if not reveal outright, the rules and logic that govern the plots that follow. As futurists Stackelberg and McDowell argue, storyworlds such as these 'provide detailed contextual rule sets that develop a larger reality' (2015: 25–6). Even the opening of 'Hansel and Gretel' shades in enough detail for a mental picture, with each line adding sharpness and clarity, producing a subtle illusion of reality and a framework for understanding the actions that occur in the story. This is the kind of work that even the most ambiguous settings can perform, and it is why we begin with this domain: because before we have a *how* and *who*, we often need a *what* and *where*.

Storyworlds constitute more than just the set dressing for events. They encompass the context, the time frame, the rules of the game and the interlocking systems which shape and constrain those who live in that world and what they can do. When a world has been built effectively, it can be extraordinarily powerful. The great fantasy writer J. R. R. Tolkien describes how imaginary worlds can enchant their readers, possessing 'realism and immediacy beyond the compass of any human mechanism' ([1945] 2008: 63–4). New media theorists describe this enchantment as *conceptual immersion* (Wolf 2012: 48), the phenomenon of experiencing another world aesthetically. To immerse yourself in an imaginary world, then, is not only to understand it but also to form a vivid attachment to it.

For many Story Thinkers, the first step to engaging in imaginative work will be understanding and immersing themselves in the landscape of their own knowledge and the problem they want to solve. Some activities aligned with this domain include:

- mapping out a 'problem space': elements of the environment such as influences, affordances and constraints that shape scenarios and restrict feasible actions (see Newell and Simon 1972);

- situating a research problem in an imaginatively constructed but realistic system to see how it might change that system;

- imagining alternative environments and contexts in which a research problem might be introduced;

- creating imaginary worlds to identify preferable changes in a system and plan transitions toward them;

- exploring snapshots of a future world to discover how current trends may evolve;

- co-creating storyworlds to build a sense of cohort and shared commitment.

In the discussion that follows, we outline specific principles and strategies that SFF writers use to create effective and immersive storyworlds and we draw attention to the ways you can adapt these for collaborative problem solving in Story Labs. In doing so, we lay the groundwork for future chapters which discuss plotting potential storylines or scenarios (Chapter 2), inventing and situating characters within a storyworld (Chapter 3) and binding all these elements through transformative language (Chapter 4).

Conceptualizing storyworlds

SFF writers have a term for the complex and enjoyable work they do when crafting speculative settings: worldbuilding. Creating an immersive storyworld involves fusing real-world research with informed speculation, typically by doing the cognitive work we have discussed in our introduction: firstly, finding an initial starting point or entry into the world (often by asking, 'What if?'), next, by extrapolating outward and making logical inferences from what has already been decided (by asking, 'What else?') and lastly by using critical judgement to evaluate each step and test its fitness for purpose (by asking, 'What for?').

Scale and complexity

Just as systems can be large or small, so too can storyworlds. Tolkien's Middle Earth is a world, but so too is the Ares 3 landing site where the stranded astronaut Mark Watney spends most of his time in Andy Weir's 2014 novel *The Martian*. But – if we flip perspectives for a moment – so is Bilbo Baggins's little house in the Shire, and so is the whole of the planet Mars. The size of the world – where its borders end – is a matter of focus. Understanding this basic point enables us to make some less obvious points:

- *Storyworlds are specific, not interchangeable.* When you change the details of the world, you change what actions can take place within it.

- *Storyworlds are enmeshed, not discrete.* While they may contain their own internal logic, that logic will always point outward to other worlds.

- *Storyworlds are not static, but are in a state of flux.* They have a history that shapes the present and anticipates future trajectories.

- *Storyworlds scale.* As a worldbuilder it is up to you to decide how much of the world you wish to describe and in what granularity of detail.

Why does this last point matter? Because it is easy for writers to get lost in their imaginary worlds: to make maps, to invent or document languages and cultures, to explore complex histories and geopolitics. The vast majority of us do not have the luxury to create worlds for the sheer pleasure of doing so (though that pleasure certainly exists). Rather we do so for particular purposes and we adopt strategies, as this chapter discusses, that are suitable for those purposes. As a worldbuilder it is perfectly reasonable to write HERE BE DRAGONS over some sections of the map. An incomplete map is not a failure of worldbuilding but rather a success of focus. The best writers shade in what they need, only as they need it.

Even simple worlds can become more complex over time because they invite energized and persistent participation: through reading and imaginatively filling in the gaps, through interactive platforms (such as gaming) and amateur activity (such as fan fiction). Samutina argues that fan fiction writers, for example, are 'not only the inhabitants of fictional worlds and interactive media environments, but the active transformers of their borders' (2016: 435) when they create new scenarios inside the fictional universes they admire. This is also how activists use worldbuilding. Inspired by the science fiction writer Octavia Butler, adrienne maree brown and Walidah Imarisha describe how community organizers 'dedicate their lives to creating and envisioning another world, or many other worlds,' inviting 'movement builders to be able to claim the vast space of possibility, to be birthing visionary stories' (2015: 3). As a pleasurable and immersive activity, then, worldbuilding can be a powerful tool for co-creation, collaboration and problem solving.

As we navigate and experiment with storyworlds we begin to understand the rules and relationships that govern them and as we build our own storyworlds, we realize these rules and relationships are also subject to change. Storyworlds then can guide us in directing and improving systems and planning transitions toward preferable futures. Zaidi argues they can act as prototypes for complete and coherent system states, technologies, and values. The systemic nature of storyworlds allows us to repeatedly mine a world for new ideas and insights, with different stakeholders deriving different value. For instance, an entrepreneur may look to *Blade Runner* for product innovation, a transportation specialist for city planning, or a lawyer for human rights implications. Robust worlds provide endless strategic possibilities because they are difficult to exhaust.

(2019: 20)

Many science fiction writers embed a goal of moving toward preferable futures in their own creative projects. Author Neal Stephenson formed Project Hieroglyph to spur innovation by imagining hopeful futures (Finn and Wylie 2021). Kim Stanley Robinson's compelling near-future novel *Ministry for the Future* (2020) narrates a fictional attempt by a newly created United Nations (UN) agency to use policy action to mitigate the climate change's worst effects, grounded in scientific accuracy and supported by non-fiction descriptions of history and social science. Although some of the natural disasters Robinson describes are truly harrowing, the novel itself remains optimistic: deftly avoiding the trap of either uncritical utopia or unswervingly bleak dystopia. It was so influential that Barack Obama named it one of his favourite reads of the year and Robinson himself was invited to attend the 2021 United Nations Climate Change Conference.

Logic and internal consistency

Much worldbuilding advice comes from the central principle that good storyworlds are internally consistent (Wolf 2012: 33). Internal consistency allows worldbuilders to extrapolate in both directed and improvisational ways. The author of the mega-bestselling *Song of Ice and Fire* series, George R. R. Martin, describes Tolkien's directed approach as that of an architect: 'The architects plan everything ahead of time, like an architect building a house …

They have the whole thing designed and blueprinted out before they even nail the first board up' (Flood 2011). He contrasts this with his own improvisational approach, that of a gardener. Gardeners, he says, 'dig a hole, drop in a seed and water it … as the plant comes up and they water it, they don't know how many branches it's going to have, they find out as it grows' (ibid.). Both approaches use the same process of extrapolation, but architects tend to prefer doing the work up front with a clear vision in mind for their world while gardeners tend to be led by the story itself and the prompts it suggests. Following the internal logic of worldbuilding can often lead you in startling directions, where a writer, in Terry Pratchett's words, 'appl[ies] logic in places where it wasn't intended to exist' (cited in Piepenbring 2015), for example, by exploring the logistics systems the Tooth Fairy might use to haul her goods around.

While internal consistency can be one way of judging whether the extrapolative decisions you have made are fit for purpose (as you ask yourself 'What for?'), it isn't always the best way. M. John Harrison once called the worldbuilding of many of his contemporaries 'the great clomping foot of nerdism' (2007). He preferred in his work to highlight incongruities and gaps in the logic that seems to undergird his readers' conception of reality, and he excoriated SFF works for creating substitute realities 'so lavish, so detailed and so long that they provide a complete "world" for their audience' (1975: 212). He saw these stories as providing 'some more or less easily grasped handle by which to pick up the universe' (ibid.). We argue that there can be real value in simplifying a storyworld so that chosen elements come into focus, but we also take Harrison's point that this simplification can come with its own dangers.

But lavish worlds are also often layered worlds. When it comes to depth and complexity, we find it useful to highlight several aspects of storyworlds described by author Jeff VanderMeer:

Much like the individual people who live there, the real world is layered and complex. In a city like London modern buildings exist next to those from the 1600s, with St. Paul's Cathedral right next to a skyscraper. Similarly, you might in some regions of the world see a farmer using oxen to plow his field while he talks on a cell phone. Places and cultures change over time, and often the past walks side by side with the present. Be careful not to reduce your worldview down to something monolithic that ignores this fact, or you may experience a slow creep toward other generalities (and banalities).

(2013: 225)

Here VanderMeer suggests good storyworlds ought to exhibit varying levels of 'consistent inconsistency' (ibid.): an apparently homogenous storyworld may have multiple levels to it or may have elements that seem incongruous at first glance. Two other pieces of advice flow from this. Firstly, storyworlds should be heterogenous and multicultural and, secondly, they should contain multiple operational realities: the natural rifts between the perspectives of different people who experience those worlds in different ways and are subject to different pressures, influences and constraints within them. We address the topic of imaginary people in more detail in Chapter 3 but we recognize that in many cases difference in perspective is not simply a matter of characterization. Rather, it is a function of the complexity of the worlds themselves.

The novum and its totalizing effects

The literary critic Darko Suvin argues the process of worldbuilding distinguishes the poetics of speculative fiction from other forms of literature. At its heart, speculative fiction takes some new idea (what he calls a *novum*, which could be a novel technology, concept, process or event) and explores the 'totalizing effects' it has on its storyworld ([1979] 2016: 80). Many writers start with a core concept or question, situating that concept in the real world (as they understand it) and then following the logic incrementally through time to create a vision of a society changed by events, people, and their tools and technologies. For example, Nancy Kress's *Beggars in Spain* (1993) imagines what the future might be like if certain children were genetically engineered so that they don't sleep. She extrapolates a possible storyworld that sees society increasingly divided between those with the secondary benefits (more productivity, higher IQ) and those without.

Other writers approach their work by observing phenomena in the world around them and asking 'What else?' to anticipate the future. In an interview with *The New Yorker*, William Gibson describes how he first coined the term 'cyberspace', foreshadowing the developments that would come in the tech industry decades later. In the late 1970s, he was watching kids in video arcades and noticing how they moved while they played, as if they were living inside the game (Rothman 2019). He began jotting down words that might describe the space behind the screen, experimenting with 'infospace' and 'dataspace' before finally settling on 'cyberspace' as the perfect word to encapsulate his idea (we discuss the value of selecting the right word for the right idea in Chapter 4). His novel *Neuromancer*, which fleshed out the idea in more detail, described it as: 'A consensual hallucination experienced daily by billions of legitimate operators, in every nation … A graphic representation of data abstracted from the banks of every computer in the human system. Unthinkable complexity. Lines of light ranged in the nonspace of the mind, clusters and constellations of data. Like city lights, receding' (1984: 51). But 'cyberspace' – a *novum* in Suvin's framing – is not a free-floating concept; it is enmeshed in the novel's storyworld, which develops its aesthetics and the system into which it fits. Gibson uses this totalizing world-system, with its colourful array of characters from different walks of life with different motivations and backstories, to explore how 'the Street finds its own uses for things – uses the manufacturers never imagined' (1986: 215). This shows us that becoming a good worldbuilder requires observation skills: noticing details, thinking about how they fit together, staying tuned to signals. It also involves, as we have hinted, being able to move across different scales.

Strategies for inhabiting

In the previous section, we laid out a conceptual framework for understanding the features of imaginary storyworlds. In this section, we discuss techniques that translate the writerly craft of worldbuilding to real-world problem solving. This is an area where our work bears some resemblance to futures studies, the interdisciplinary field that explores and analyses possible futures to help individuals, organizations and societies make more informed decisions in the present. Although SFF and futures studies share some overlap, we recognize there is a longstanding tension with some degree of mutual suspicion (e.g. Miles 1993 and Marshall, Jennings and Anderton 2023). The aims of futures studies include understanding the drivers of change, anticipating future challenges and opportunities, and developing strategies to navigate and shape the future (Masini 1993). Its practitioners use a variety of methods, including scenario planning, trend analysis and modelling to enhance strategic foresight. Our approach is both broader and looser, rooted in the understanding that creative methods may make use of strictly plausible future storyworlds as well as those that deliberately explore unusual or implausible premises to shed light on hidden assumptions or to explore aspects of a politically sensitive situation best approached obliquely.

Worldbuilding – like many of the skills in creative writing that we discuss in this book – is inherently accretive. One detail of the world will naturally suggest the next, as you extrapolate using the system of logic you have established for your world, asking yourself questions as they occur to you and then offering answers that resonate or make sense with what has already been suggested. In practice, this process of questioning and revising is crucial because a worldbuilder doesn't want to build blindly. Some avenues may be more useful to explore while others may be too farfetched. In fact, if premises are built into a world that are difficult to justify or which some observers find too unrealistic, the subsequent premises flowing on from them will likewise be contaminated by disbelief.

Below we offer a range of techniques for getting started or finding an anchor for your storyworld, a prompt that allows you to begin asking questions, as well as some suggestions for how to deal with common challenges that arise when co-creating new worlds.

Asking what if

Asking a literal 'What if?' question is an easy way to start. This approach sets you up to explore a series of consequences. This might involve starting with the real world as it exists today, with the idea that totalizing changes to the world will filter through as the plot unfolds. When opting for this approach, you may find it useful to ask a series of 'What if?' questions in order to put multiple potential changes to the system in place: for example, what if the Metaverse achieves significant market penetration *and* we are confronting a global climate crisis? Often using several prompts together will produce more interesting answers, though too many may cause you to lose focus.

Finding an interesting or unusual problem

Terry Pratchett, the author of the beloved *Discworld* novels, is reported to have opened a discussion on worldbuilding by asking, 'How does the shit get out, and the clean water get in?' (cited in Scullard 2012). This is obviously an unusual starting point for a fantasy world but, by building the city of Ankh-Morpork from the river upward to answer this question, he foregrounded an entirely different set of details and mechanics than if he had begun with the question, 'How does magic work in the Discworld?'

Displacing a problem

If you know a research problem well, it can be useful to transplant it into an entirely new context. Jaroslav Kalfař's *Spaceman of Bohemia* (2017) imagines what might happen if humanity made first contact with an alien species, but the space programme was controlled by Czechoslovakia: a combination *The Guardian* described as 'an episode of *Star Trek* [crashing] into Milan Kundera's *The Joke*' (Fischer 2017). Margaret Atwood's *The Handmaid's Tale* (1985) likewise explores what might happen if America were run as a totalitarian theocratic republic. This approach defamiliarizes the problem by allowing the constraints and possibilities of the new setting to generate fresh insights.

Templating

Tolkien's Middle Earth was heavily informed and inflected by his work as a medievalist, and aspects of the cultures in his world clearly draw inspiration from Norse, Celtic and Anglo-Saxon history and myth. Likewise, George R. R. Martin's sprawling political fantasy series *Song of Ice and Fire* echoes his research into the War of the Roses (but with dragons!). In each case we see what Ryan calls a strategy of 'minimal departure' (1980) in which worldbuilders signal they are using some template for their world (often 'the world as we know it' within science fiction) and only marking out significant points of divergence.

Templating can develop worlds that dramatize aspects of our own world that we may be habituated toward. Award-winning fantasy writer N. K. Jemisin, for example, has convincingly argued that issues such as systemic racism can be the 'necessary fuel' (2014) for alternative worlds and shouldn't be ignored even if they are uncomfortable. You can mix and match templates, or layer them on top of one another. Pratchett's city of Ankh-Morpork, for example, is templated upon both a generic fantasy world *and* the United Kingdom.

Working with trends

This strategy is common within SF, which has developed formulae to help worldbuilders identify points of divergence: exaggeration (distorting current trends), inversion (reversing current trends) and extension (extrapolating current trends) (Samuelson 1993: 194). This resonates with how futurists use trends, precursors and scenario analyses to extrapolate on scientific data in informed ways (Castillo 2009).

Beginning with character

Some writers prefer to work at the local: not the view *of* the world but the view *from* the world. They dip into the viewpoint of characters who look, hear, touch and learn about their environment, bringing the general contours of the world into a sharper specificity. If you've already developed a character this may be a good way to get started.

Artefacts

Artefacts from another world can also anchor you in the local. This is the particular focus of design fiction, a practice that explores and evaluates future scenarios through the study of imaginary objects with obvious overlaps with science fiction. These objects are like 'props of conversations that help speculate, reflect and imagine, even without words' (Bleecker 2009). For example, we might imagine a communications device from the future and then interrogate what assumptions it seems to express. Does it use a screen? A blue-light hologram? Does it speak in the voice of a best friend or with a strangely artificial robotic tone? Objects may be one focus for this technique, but others exist, including headlines or newspapers from the future.

Literalized extended metaphor

Writers often represent some aspect of the contemporary world they wish to explore via a metaphor, and then treat that metaphor as if it had force. For example, Naomi Alderman's *The Power* (2016) uses the ability to produce electrical shocks as a metaphor or stand-in for other forms of physical strength. The novel can be read literally as an exploration of a new biological adaptation but it can also be read metaphorically as a discussion of gender and power. Literalized metaphors (which we discuss more in Chapter 4) may present challenges for some worldbuilders who prefer to stay grounded in pure realism but can also be usefully estranging, allowing you to map features of the real world into a fictional space where you can follow the logic in unusual and provocative ways.

Challenges

While the approaches we have outlined harness the strengths of worldbuilding, it is also worth noting some of the limitations when using these skills to solve real-world problems. These include:

- worlds too big or too small for the research problem you want to explore;

- world lacking logical connections between elements or missing something important, making them unfit for your purpose;

- worlds with little variation (purely utopian, purely dystopian);

- worlds that unintentionally replicate the unspoken assumptions about the logic of the 'real world' (particularly with respect to gender, race, ability and class);

- worlds too overloaded with detail for collaborators to master and use with ease;

- worlds with too little detail, forcing collaborators to ask for more information or invent it themselves, instead of progressing with other kinds of imaginative work;

- worlds that ignore, sideline or downplay the perspectives of the people who might be affected by the group's research;

- future worlds whose logic is purely incremental, neglecting the possibility of 'surprise, discontinuities, reversals, tipping points, etc' (Bode and Dietrich 2013: 100).

It's worth being aware of these challenges because worldbuilding may be an area requiring extra attention. If the storyworld is not fit for purpose, these issues are likely to contaminate any further explorations of plot and character grounded in the world, preventing collaborators from suspending their disbelief.

If your storyworld is too homogenous, try the following tactics to create texture and variety:

- seeding in additional prompts and looking for connections between them;

- breaking the expected logic in one area of the world and seeing what happens;

- returning to a prompt and deliberately choosing a less conventional response;

- ensuring you bring diverse perspectives into the process of worldbuilding;

- moving from the systemic level to the local and adopting the perspective of an outsider.

Building upon this last point, as you develop your world it can be useful to shift your perspective from time to time by asking how an aspect of the setting might be experienced in a day-to-day lived sense. In military decision-making, the phrase 'Big Hands, Small Maps' refers to the problem of generals making decisions using maps that lack the resolution to show how the land actually lies. That is, they might have a systemic view but lack the ability to see local detail and the level of lived experience. But for anyone working at an operational level, this sort of detail is vital. As writers we constantly switch from the big picture to the local and back again in order to find the edges of our world, add depth, and contain and situate our stories in a meaningful way.

Conclusion

Many speculative writers tend to begin new creative projects by either focusing on the world first (the approach of J. R. R. Tolkien and others like him who draw countless maps and craft detailed histories until their worlds take on considerable depth and texture) or character first (the approach of M. John Harrison who subordinates the world to the needs of the story, leaving much hinted at without being fully defined). Whether your approach is maximalist or minimalist, it's important to recognize that settings are always more than just backdrops. They impose rules and restrictions on characters and determine how their plots can unfold. When problem-solving in teams, worldbuilding can be a pleasurable and powerful tool for collaboration because it immerses collaborators in a process of co-creation. More than that, credible, internally consistent and purpose-built settings can help researchers ask questions about the present contexts of their challenges or generate scenarios that look forward into the future or indeed sideways into other possible contexts.

The strange and fantastical settings of SFF novels can also help researchers think through real-world problems. Future-focused settings act as logical extensions of our present reality – *if things keep going as they are, then this or this or even* that *could feasibly happen* – and are often more accessible and familiar to researchers, particularly those from science, technology, engineering and mathematics (STEM) backgrounds. Yet fantasy worlds offer their own pleasures and practical contributions. They grant Story Thinkers the opportunity to displace problems and extend metaphors. Settings like Middle Earth or Westeros or Narnia may be sufficiently removed from our reality (by time and space, the inclusion of supernatural or magical elements, impossible climates and locales, etc.) to offer intellectual and emotional buffers for those who feel constrained in how they imagine. Even simply using the names of these settings can give collaborators a cognitive 'get out of jail free' card. This is one reason why, when working on Defence problems where we're restricted from using real-world place names, we ourselves often name locations after kingdoms from Middle Earth. Some settings such as the fantastical landscape of N. K. Jemisin's *Broken Earth Trilogy* (2015–17) can also function allegorically, nestling contemporary issues such as racism within their confines so they can be explored at a safe distance. The stakes can feel lower when economic or environmental or enchanted disasters loom in a fictional world – so collaborators feel less pressure to 'get the right answer'. The beauty of these worlds, of course, is that we can break and rebuild them as many times as we need, without risk or real-world repercussions.

PROJECT URSULA: A CASE STUDY IN USING IMAGINATIVE WORLDS TO ANCHOR SCENARIOS

The project

Project Ursula was a funded collaboration between the University of Queensland and the Defence Science and Technology Group (DSTG). We were tasked with designing a collaborative workshop that would bring experts together from different disciplines to produce scenarios imagining how virtual existence technologies such as augmented reality, virtual real estate and the Metaverse might develop over the next ten to twenty years.

This kind of workshop, which focuses on technological foresight (that is, exploring possibilities for the uses of technologies in the future), is a natural fit for our Story Thinking framework. We took Ursula K. Le Guin for our namesake because her approach to SFF was grounded in sociology. Rather than focusing on technology first, as many of her contemporaries were inclined to do, she speculated about human behaviours and cultures. We wanted to capture this use of worldbuilding to help our collaborators break out of their disciplinary silos and the ways of thinking habituated within them.

The challenge

Strategic foresight workshops often take a methodical approach to generating scenarios. For example, many businesses engage in long-term strategic planning by using a STEEPLE model, which examines various parameters of an environment (social, technological, economic, environmental, political, legal and ethical) as 'a kind of radar to scan the world systematically and signal the new, the unexpected, the major and the minor' (Brown and Weiner 1985: ix; see also More, Probert and Phaal 2015). This approach has the benefit of being exhaustive, prompting participants to look at scenario parameters they might otherwise ignore. Unfortunately, it's also time-consuming and, we argue, less likely to produce edge cases and second-order effects because there are no mechanisms in place to force elements in the system to collide.

We wanted to draw on some of the strengths of the STEEPLE model, which has obvious overlaps with some of the strategies writers use when creating new settings. At the same time, we wanted our use of worldbuilding to prompt participants to think in unexpected ways. These are the questions we asked ourselves:

- How big should the world our participants were examining be? Could the scenarios be situated anywhere in the world? How specific were we going to be about the timeframe of ten to twenty years?
- How many worlds did we want to explore? Did we want each scenario to take place in a world with different parameters or should the scenarios all be set within a world with the same parameters, showing a breadth of possibilities?
- How realistic should the worlds be? What mechanisms were we going to put in place to maintain that realism?
- How would the initial parameters of the worlds be decided? Would the worlds be co-created by participants during the session or would we the facilitators decide on each of the parameters in advance?

The approach

We began with a simple seeding exercise ('What if?'). We took three of the STEEPLE domains (environmental, social and economic) and created a question for each:

- In ten years, how might climate change action affect Australia?
- In ten years, which groups and/or nation(s) will have the most power?
- What might happen to Australia's economy over the next ten years?

The questions were open-ended but the timeframe of the exercise and the central geographic focus provided useful constraints. Participants had two minutes to suggest responses before we polled them to see which they wished to explore further. Many answers naturally followed the extrapolative formulae we discussed earlier: exaggerations, inversions and extensions of contemporary trends. By polling the group, we allowed them the opportunity to exercise their own judgement ('What for?') in determining which trends they felt were realistic and fit for purpose. The top two answers to each question were taken as anchors for the world, giving six in total.

In the following exercise, we divided the cohort into small groups and gave each a set of prompts to aid them imagining a scenario within that world. For example:

- A group of people does not have access to virtual existence technologies. Why? How might they gain access or what sort of rival system might they turn to instead?
- Virtual existence technologies raise new questions about sustainability. What real-world considerations are being neglected? What will happen if they are not addressed?
- A grassroots movement arises to expand the laws governing virtual existence technologies. What do they want to protect? Who might oppose this law and why?

These scenarios fleshed out one or several aspects of the world ('What else?'). The result was that each scenario was linked by a common thread of imagination but remained distinct enough to reveal different aspects of the co-created future. The workshop was ultimately a success, resulting in a number of tangible outcomes: a report to government which included the scenarios we generated and their accompanying analysis (Anderton et al. 2023), a methodological paper (Marshall, Jennings et al. 2023), and a detailed facilitator's guide circulated internally at the DSTG.

2

Envision: Epic wins and nasty surprises

Introduction

The day I found the body on the beach was the first fine weather since Patrick had left me.

This opening line for a story – for demonstration purposes only; it is not taken from a real novel – encapsulates the three elements of story we laid out in the Introduction. The *context* (or setting) may be a beachside location, the *character* may be mourning a lost love, but it is the central *conflict* – and the plot that elaborates it – that hooks readers, getting them emotionally invested in how things will turn out. Has there been a murder? A shipwreck? Oh, wait, *is the body Patrick's??* It's unusual to find a body on the beach (substitute 'body' with 'seashell' and the line loses all its interest), and so our imaginations catch on it and cling … like seaweed on a washed-up body. Certainly the narrator's backstory – the protagonist's life in the sleepy seaside town, the whole sad affair with Patrick – may create interest, maybe even make us fall in love with the story, but, for sheer stickiness of attention, nothing works like conflict.

A story's inciting incident – the body on the beach – introduces the chief source of narrative conflict in the story, upsetting the world's equilibrium and giving the protagonist an immediate problem to solve. This is what conflicts do in stories: they force choices and create action. In real life, we may ignore problems, but the rules of story are that when a character has a problem, she must respond. In fiction, if a character ignores a problem, then typically the problem will worsen until she is *forced* to act (someone *else* stumbles across the body and discovers a connection to *her*). When she does respond, every solution the character applies to the problem enmeshes her further: she solves the problem only partially or not at all, she alerts potential enemies to her exploitable weaknesses, she is compelled to enlist allies and must struggle to acquire them, and so on. This playing out of problem, solution, further problem, further solution gives a story forward motion over time.

But great plots aren't just for storytellers. Story Thinkers can use the power of plotting to envision possibilities linked by chains of cause and effect. In this chapter we provide a conceptual framework for thinking about several key elements of plotting: conflict, causality and structure. We also provide some practical strategies for calibrating probable, possible and implausible pathways, and managing utopian and dystopian thinking. Some conceptual approaches aligned with this domain include:

- extrapolating multiple possibilities based on information at hand to generate ideas;

- understanding the role of conflict and threat in creating compelling, attention-grabbing narratives, effective for wargaming or scenario planning;

- following chains of cause and effect with key stopping points along the way to understand how systems change over time or events develop;

- building up detailed scenarios around tipping points and crises alongside slow-burn changes such as demographics;

- brainstorming potential divergence points and how they might positively or negatively affect outcomes;

- flirting with the implausible through bold 'moonshot' thinking, or imagining 'black swan' events;

- imagining worst-case scenarios then working backwards to find weaknesses in systems or areas for risk mitigation.

In our discussion so far, we have emphasized the role characters play in plotting – their choices, the problems they face. This is because writers typically use characters as focalizers when creating the action in a story, a point we elaborate in Chapter 3. As our opening demonstrates, one of the simplest methods for generating plot possibilities is to imagine what a character might do and what consequences might follow. But settings also have obvious impacts on how events unfold. People and ideas can shape world events but so too can the particular pressures created by harsh landscape, limited resources and contested territorial boundaries (Marshall 2016). Crucially, the space of possibility changes from moment to moment as the situation shifts. Living through a global pandemic certainly taught us that actions unthinkable one day can become commonplace six months later as people come to accept a new operational reality. Sometimes, only by exploring the journey – the critical pathway that links events – can we understand what is really possible.

Conceptualizing plots

Conflict, causality and extrapolation

We need to disambiguate a number of terms before we can begin our discussion of the craft of plotting. Morris and Van Cleave describe plot as 'a series of events' (2021: 18), while Gottschall notes that plot proceeds from a conflict: 'If there is no knotty problem, there is no story' (2012: 49). Nick Harkaway builds on this by proposing that conflict, or simple opposition, can create potential energy in stories (2021) because it creates possibilities. So we see already that conflict and plot are not identical: conflict provides drama and tension while plot provides structure. In this section, we are interested in how conflict drives plot, introducing tension, obstacles and challenges that propel the narrative forward, structured by causality.

What do we mean by causality? Chatman suggests that plot events 'are not simply linear – they have a cause-and-effect relationship' (1978: 45). One event leads to another, creating a chain reaction that shapes the story's progression. This is a key aspect that the popularized use of 'story' gets wrong: a persistent lay understanding of story is that it implies a list of things that happened when it is actually so much more. As E. M. Forster noted in *Aspects of the Novel*, plot is 'a narrative of events, the emphasis falling on causality' and as such 'demands intelligence and memory' to make sense of those chains of cause and effect (1927: 116). Echoing this, Jon-K Adams argues for narrative as 'an act of explanation' which links events to 'account for what has happened' (1989: 149). Talking through stories – telling them to others, pulling them apart, questioning them – allows us to make sense of the world and decide not only what *should* happen next, but *why*. In an interview with us, writers Claire S. E. Cooney and Carlos Hernandez noted that 'we tell each other stories every day, we narrativize all the time. It's how we shape our world, how we make sense of the world, and how we prepare for future problems' (2022). This focus on sensemaking shows the domain's relevance across fields, from science education (e.g. White 1993; Passmore, Gouvea and Giere 2014) to sociological work on collective action (e.g. Andersen, Ravn and Thomson 2020).

Understanding the role of causality in plotting makes the work of envisioning easier: in the beginning a character has a problem that forces them to act and others to respond. All a writer needs to ask is *if this happens then what next*? And *then what else*? Importantly, though, the causal connections allow writers to move in either direction, extrapolating forward or backward. Some writers imagine a story's end-state and find the pathway to reach it while others begin with a crisis that sets things into motion and then trace the logic forward.

Causality also allows writers to fill in the gaps when they have different levels of information about either the end point they are trying to reach or the stopping points along the way. Author Kelly Robson says, 'I know where it's going to end and I know a few points along the way' (2018); Alyx Dellamonica however 'sit[s] down with almost no idea what I'm going to write every morning when I'm drafting a new book' (2022). An article by writers Sisterson and Nugent, where they hash out the debate between 'plotters' (those who like to plan their stories ahead of writing them) and 'pantsers' (those who start writing and fly by the seat of their pants), describes their disagreement over the best method this way: 'if I was going to build a house, I wouldn't just start laying bricks' (Sisterson, Spain and Nugent 2021: 16) versus 'my imagination is more fired by not knowing than by knowing' (2021: 17). Importantly for Story Thinkers, both orientations offer ways to envision how a story might progress. Improvisation helps writers see what happens if they choose a particular starting point and work forward, calibrating along the way and testing the causal links, while planning in advance allows them to visualize a desired end point and explore the progressions and transitions needed in order to reach it.

Structure, transition points and temporality

Many writers discuss the progression of plots in terms of 'points' on a timeline, moments when characters make key decisions, or events that come to a head. Writers arrange these points for particular effects, paying attention to how they modulate tension by introducing and resolving complications. If a story piles too many setbacks onto one another, the reader can lose interest or develop a sense of fatalism, while endless success can diffuse any sense of jeopardy – no one wants to see someone winning all the time. Jane

McGonigal (2010) sees a similar pattern in the structured difficulty of video games, patterns which she argues can be usefully repurposed to support real-world cooperative problem-solving. Too many obstacles can make us feel overwhelmed, frustrated or cynical, while the right level of difficulty – one that pushes the limits of capability – inspires collaboration, motivating people to do something that matters and encouraging them to try again after failure. The pattern of successes and failures, or, more broadly, the pattern of events, shapes our experience of a journey, not just its destination.

Our experience of a story then is not just intellectual but also emotional: this too comes down to the careful selection and arrangement of events (McKee 1999: 33). Wilkins describes how the right plot structure can produce 'intense gratification', the feeling of 'wanting to stay lost in the story forever and yet at the same time finding ourselves unable to stop turning the pages and racing towards the resolution' (2012: 47). These experiences are rooted in the way that stories affect our brain chemistry, with dramatic or tense events generating cortisol (Popova 2012). Indeed, a study that mapped brain activity to story structure showed that rising action provokes more brain activity than the simple introduction of story elements, proving plot keeps audiences engaged (Grady, Schmälzle and Baldwin 2022: 17).

Many writers have proposed basic story structures to pattern events for particular emotional impact or sensemaking. The German playwright Gustav Freytag used a 'pyramid' to describe the structure of a drama, emphasizing the rising action, climax and denouement (Kercheval 2003: 83). Kurt Vonnegut (2005), on the other hand, advanced eight essential story structures (e.g. Man in Hole, Boy Meets Girl, Cinderella, From Bad to Worse, Creation Story, etc.). As we argue in Chapter 6, none of these models are universal and there are dangers in thinking about them as if they are. Practically, though, Western SFF novels tend to conform to a simple structure we have found helpful in our Story Labs. Initially, the inciting event sets the characters and plot into motion. It introduces the central conflict, destabilizes the status quo and gives the protagonist a problem to solve or a situation demanding response. Two transition points follow (one around 25 per cent through the novel and one around 75 per cent through the novel). Wilkins calls these the 'gear changes in the narrative structure' (2012: 45) where characters face critical decisions, confront obstacles and experience significant shifts in their trajectories. Finally, the climax brings the conflict to a head where the central issue demands resolution, often in a showdown of opposing forces or a momentous decision, with the protagonist needing to bring all their skills and resources to bear in order to succeed.

One of the benefits of this structure is that it can scale across decades (such as in Kim Stanley Robinson's *Red Mars* (1992) which follows the first forty years of terraforming and colonization) or a single pivotal day (Stephen King's *The Long Walk* (1979)). This brings us to another important point. In stories, narrative structure plays out over time, which is one reason this domain is particularly useful for futures thinking. Most stories proceed chronologically but some may adopt what Jarva calls a 'more complicated chronotope' (2014: 13). An example of this is Martin Amis's *Time's Arrow* (1991), narrated backwards in time but with all of the sense of rising tension that a forward-narrated story might hold. The relationship between the forward motion of plot and the chronology of story, then, is not necessarily identical. Even stories that largely proceed linearly make use of devices such as *analepsis* (recounting an event from a different position in time, often in the form of a flashback) to help readers make sense of how a character, situation or setting's history may shape its future. But understanding chronology is useful because it shows that when characters or systems change, these changes occur over time: sometimes driven by incremental shifts, sometimes by crises, tipping points and reversals.

One aspect of plotting that brings together an understanding of causality and its relationship to both transition points and chronology is the 'jonbar hinge', a term coined in the 1930s science fiction novel *The Legion of Time* by Jack Williamson (Hellekson 2009). The term refers to an historical moment imagined differently, a point of divergence from known and largely accepted timelines, from which an author can extrapolate a story that explores unthought-of possibilities. For example, Richard Harris's *Fatherland* (1992) imagines a version of Berlin if Hitler won the Second World War, complete with Albert Speer's epic Volkshalle dome; while Kim Stanley Robinson's *The Years of Rice and Salt* (2002) speculates on a version of Europe where the Black Plague wiped out enough of the population for Eastern cultures to invade and build their empires.

Time travel stories commonly use jonbar hinges: Desmond Warzel's short story 'Wikihistory' takes place on the Members' Forum for the International Association of Time Travelers and follows the attempts of a series of new members who visit Berlin in 1936 (and indeed at various points in the historical timeline) to assassinate Adolf Hitler. As long-time poster BigChill writes in the story, 'Everybody kills Hitler on their first trip. I did. It always gets fixed within a few minutes, what's the harm?' (2011). We've found this Hitler-killing reference point so accessible that we have used it for the title of one of our exercises for generating multiple scenarios, discussed in Chapter 7. Ultimately, the jonbar hinge allows writers to imagine divergence points, following new chains of possibilities at the level of the character-as-meaningful-actor or the world-as-system-prone-to-influence-and-change.

Strategies for envisioning

According to Jarva, narratives have always played a role in imagining the future (forecasting) but also influencing and inspiring people to act (2014). When put into practice, this envision domain asks us to think about how Story Thinkers evaluate future forecasts and plan to reach desirable outcomes (Beach 2009) and improve research and development decisions (Rutten, Dorée and Halman 2013). The domain also intersects with elements of wargaming and scenario planning, both of which share a common objective to prepare organizations and decision-makers for a range of possible future outcomes. Wargaming does this by simulating competitive or adversarial situations, often in a military context, to assess and enhance strategic decision-making under pressure, while scenario planning involves creating and analysing plausible future scenarios to better understand potential risks and opportunities. This kind of work can be done by progressively advancing current trends, as we discuss in our case study, or back-casting, which involves imagining a future state (either preferable or cautionary) and then mapping out the transition points necessary to link it to the present. Our Story Labs often incorporate aspects of game playing and scenario planning with a particular focus on plotting.

We have noted that when we ask creative teams to imagine the future, they often gravitate toward dystopias. Dystopian thinking can be very useful in a pre-mortem, an activity in which you imagine a worst-case scenario to learn lessons about how a system might fail. However, Harkaway (2021) argues that dystopia feels less and less relevant as media narratives about the world itself have grown more dystopian. While we may not believe in the old-school version of utopia anymore and utopian futures can be static and dull, Harkaway suggests looking for 'green shoots' of positivity for the future. Sometimes it can be useful to ban worst-case scenarios, or to give collaborators an opportunity to imagine them and then move on. Focusing on 'best-case' or 'weird-case' scenarios can produce more actionable results.

Best-case scenarios need not be utopian, though they can be inspiring. One way of developing such scenarios is moonshotting. A 'moonshot' is an idea or goal that is ambitious, exploratory and ground-breaking, so named for the moon mission of 1969. The term is now common parlance, especially in the tech sphere, for a hugely innovative, bold and potentially risky goal (Awati, Bernstein and Wigmore 2022). It is in moonshot thinking that we push the imagination into radically positive possibilities, setting an aspiration that may not be achievable, but that nonetheless might inspire bold actions and do some good even if not fully realized. A new subgenre of science fiction called 'solarpunk' captures this sense of possibility, focusing on the aesthetics and possibilities of renewable energy (Reina-Rozo 2021).

Weird-case scenarios engage more robustly with the implausible. In *The Black Swan: The Impact of the Highly Improbable*, Nassam Nicholas Taleb (2007) explains how the long-held assumption that all swans were white was upset by European explorers' first encounter with black swans in Australia. (Taleb wrongly uses the term 'before the discovery of Australia'. Australia, in fact, has one of the longest living civilizations in its Aboriginal people, who 'discovered' Australia at least 60,000 years ago.) Black swan events are difficult if not impossible to see coming as they lie outside our ordinary consensus of the world's logic. Examples often cited of black swan events include the September 11 terrorist attacks of 2001 and the global Covid-19 pandemic of 2020; though in hindsight both of these events had multiple warning signs leading up to them. In creative writing, especially SFF, exploring the implausible is a method to imagine weird-case scenarios of radical difference. Helen Marshall's debut novel *The Migration* (2019), for example, imagines a world on the verge of climate collapse, where a pandemic illness in young people turns them into strange flying creatures. While humans transforming into a never-before-seen species is highly unlikely, imagining such an event allows us to see the world in a different way, opening thinkers to new possibilities. As Michael Saler writes in his book *As If*, such fantastical scenarios 'challenge their inhabitants to see the real world as being … an imaginary construct, amenable to revision' (2012: 7).

Bearing these larger principles in mind, below we outline a range of approaches for generating plot ideas, calibrating the progression of events and constructing plausible stories using creative writing techniques.

Divergence points

Story Thinkers can generate ideas by focusing on potential 'jonbar hinges' of their own. Imagining a different version of a crucial historical turning point allows researchers to build their skills with counterfactual thinking and produce narratives that they can later reflect upon or analyse. If extrapolating on the future, exploring radical divergence points or even a different version of a widely predicted crucial turning point is a great way to generate ideas about how events might unfold.

Calibrating and sorting possibilities

Once Story Thinkers begin generating possibilities, they should calibrate them for probability and implausibility to make sure they are exploring the full range of ideas. Because probable outcomes are the most obvious and ready to hand, they can actually prove to be the biggest stumbling blocks to more imaginative thinking – sometimes you need to deliberately push beyond them, into the space of implausibility, so you can backtrack and find ideas that lie in-between. It's important to note there are multiple gradations of possibility when writing a story. Stories that cleave closely to the probable may be uninteresting or teach us nothing new, while stories where every plot choice pushes right out against the implausible might not yield useful ideas (not to mention becoming exhausting!). Good writers know this and so they tend to play with the gradations of the possible in chains of cause and effect to manage dramatic tension: they can add sudden escalations, unexpected external threats, or focus on nuanced incremental shifts to create a slow burn.

Understanding the adjacent possible

Outcomes that initially seem implausible can become more plausible as you explore the chain of events to reach them. One way to think about this is the adjacent possible, 'a kind of shadow future, hovering on the edges of the present state of things, a map of all the ways in which the present can reinvent itself' (Johnson 2010: 31). The concept of the 'adjacent possible' was introduced by scientist Stuart Kauffman (2000) to describe the set of potential innovations and possibilities that are one step away from the current state of a system. It suggests that within any given system or context, there are numerous unexplored opportunities and combinations of elements that could emerge, but they are limited to what can be reached from the existing state. In essence, the adjacent possible represents the boundary of what is currently feasible, and, as the system evolves or new elements are introduced, it expands to include new possibilities. Crucially, by working out from the present to potential future states, you can get a sense of how the space of possibility changes, with some options closing down while others emerge. This can be much harder to do from a standing start: simply starting with the present and then jumping twenty years into the future.

Changing story logic

Rather than ruling out a plot point as implausible, you can rethink the story logic that forbids something being plausible. Because plausibility relies on what we already know about the world and how people act, as well as what we think is possible, implausibility violates the internal logic of the story. Sometimes changing the logic can reveal what is required to make a scenario more plausible. This might involve introducing a new backstory for a character or changing the conditions of the world in which the story takes place. For example, imagining a billionaire's secretary rising to become a powerful dictator may immediately flag as implausible. But in a world where secretaries form a powerful guild who have secretly been working at gathering an archive of their bosses' combined secrets, this scenario is not so implausible after all.

The orthogonal and nasty surprises

Moreover, the implausible isn't necessarily the impossible in the real world: let's not forget Donald Trump served a term as President of the United States, a development an episode of *The Simpsons* imagined in 2000 but few others did. Harkaway (2021) recommends that from time to time, if a group of creative thinkers is having difficulty breaking outside the bounds of what they perceive as possible, you can introduce something completely preposterous to shake up the discussion and give the group implicit permission to be playful. In Story Thinking, the word 'implausible' should never be invoked without challenge. Imagining a unique threat nobody expects is a brilliant strategy for seeing where gaps in preparations might exist, and helps in planning for resilience and mitigation. Story Thinkers must be prepared to think wildly, even if their ideas seem silly.

Moonshots and epic wins

Imagining implausible optimistic events opens up the possibilities of a story and may inspire plausible positive action. When grappling with a problem, describing what an 'epic win' might look like can prompt questions around how that win was brought into being. What were the steps to get there? What were the probable things, the possible things and the implausible things that happened? How did they line up in a cause-and-effect sequence, and what was necessary along the way?

Challenges

These approaches show how researchers can use techniques associated with plotting to work on complex problems, but it's also worth noting some common issues. These include:

- plotting situated at the wrong scale for the problem you wish to solve (either because the timeframe is wrong or because you are focalizing at the level of the world when you need to focus on a character, or vice versa);

- plotting that drives toward conflict for the sake of drama, tension and interest, thereby missing other potential forms of progression (incremental, dialogic, collaborative, diplomatic, etc.);

- plotting over-engineered by the desires or fears of collaborators;

- plotting with too many tipping points, reversals and discontinuities, making them less credible for collaborators who wish to calibrate only to the obviously plausible;

- plots that only progress incrementally;

- plots that focus only on dystopian or utopian outcomes, without the rich possibilities of the 'weird'.

The solution for plotting often lies in calibrating particular plot points. You can try:

- deliberately shifting from incremental progressions to tipping points or vice versa, to present new possibilities;

- a plausibility check to determine if all collaborators believe a plot point is likely to advance the way the group has proposed, making note of points of dissent as potential jonbar hinges to explore alternatives;

- using dice to randomly generate the success or failure of a particular initiative or decision – we often use two dice, so outcomes are weighted as follows: 2 (critical failure); 3–6 (marginal failure); 7–11 (marginal success); 12 (critical success);

- using the characterization techniques in the next chapter to evaluate whether the behaviour of the characters in your story is realistic for the situation in which they find themselves.

In terms of extrapolating a story by envisioning plot progressions, it is important to recognize there is a difference between a thought experiment, which often only follows one dimension, and a story, which incorporates multi-dimensional holistic imagining. It's those other aspects of story that bring an event to life, providing a sense of how the world and the people who interact with the change will experience it, accept or resist it, and ultimately shape it into the next point in the causal chain. As Elizabeth Bear notes, 'I prefer to write books where the argument doesn't have a single clear answer. Because if it did, why would you need to read three hundred pages about it?' (2022).

Conclusion

Most of us are risk averse. We choose our words carefully because we can imagine how others will respond. We obey speed limits because we know the potential consequences. We (try to) delay gratification and save money for house deposits, holidays and retirement because we want to enjoy those things later in our lives. We tend to see conflict as a threat to our daily well-being – we don't want to cause friction or miss a once-in-a-lifetime chance or accidentally die – so we plot various (simple or convoluted) ways to avoid it. We think ahead.

When it comes to fiction, however, writers intentionally arrange sequences of events to create conflicts and to dramatize their consequences. We cause problems to make our characters' lives more difficult because happiness in fiction is boring. Conflicts are useful plot devices (in life as in stories) because they motivate people, forcing them to adapt and pivot when plans go awry, to strategize and think in new ways. Our task as writers is to devise plotlines that challenge characters and readers alike in purpose-built ways: to engage and test but not entirely exhaust them. In this respect, we're like video game designers calibrating the players' experience and expectations at the start of a new campaign. Are they ranked as adventurer-explorers, here for a fun storyline more than combat? Are they veterans hoping for many close calls and overwhelming boss fights? Or are they masochists who select the most punishing 'nightmare' mode, knowing they'll have to redo each level dozens of times before progressing? In all cases, the architect of each challenge must bear the audience in mind and what they hope to accomplish.

In this chapter we've explored several concepts involved in this work of envisioning and offered practical techniques and productive derailments drawn from the SFF writing toolkit that will throw thinking onto new tracks. We've argued for taking the side of the 'weird case' rather than simply the 'worst case' or 'best case' when generating new ideas and imagining nuanced and even surprising responses to complex real-world problems – for it's often in considering unexpected and unusual possibilities that we discover our most creative and constructive solutions.

FUTURE SHOCK: A CASE STUDY IN USING PLOTTING TECHNIQUES TO MITIGATE RISKS FOR HUMANITARIAN AGENCIES

The project

Numbers of forcefully displaced peoples today are already at historic record levels (more than 100 million) and projections are that these numbers will rise significantly higher in the decades to come. At the same time, new sets of digital technologies (such as AI, data collection and surveillance, digital identities or predictive analytics) are growing rapidly. For the United Nations High Commissioner for Refugees (UNHCR), this evolving 'digital humanitarian space' is already offering new opportunities, risks and dilemmas, yet the organization, as we learned, necessarily tends to focus on immediate crisis response rather than long-term analysis and planning.

Our two-day Story Lab drew scholars from a range of disciplines together to anticipate how these new sets of technologies could transform the work of the UNHCR over the next twenty years. Participants developed a series of timelines that mapped out future trajectories and explored divergence points to produce best-case, worst-case and 'weird-case' scenarios. These weren't intended to be predictions but rather they helped participants explore a range of possibilities that might inform how the UNHCR could future proof the technologies they are developing to help protect some of the world's most vulnerable populations.

The challenge

The Story Lab aimed to engage a series of experts who knew their respective fields well but had relatively little experience with traditional foresight methodologies. We wanted to adopt easy-to-understand activities that would help them understand both the technologies and their possible future use cases as well as how the world itself might develop, with threats such as climate change, conflict and technological acceleration potentially putting the agency under new pressures. Rather than approaching this challenge from the lens of worldbuilding, we focused on plotting because we felt it offered a better sense of the uncertainty of these scenarios. We weren't interested so much in end-points as we were about the possibilities that might shape them and we wanted to overcome what we felt might be a problem with participants debating the realism of the scenarios by having them make choices at critical junctures. We asked ourselves:

- How could we capture the contingency of possible futures, given that the scenarios we were interested in were likely to depend on a range of environmental, social, economic, legal and political factors?
- How could we help participants imagine the effects of more predictable long-term trends alongside black swan events and technological tipping points?
- What methods might provide a sense of plausibility to help the teams understand how we arrived at scenarios?

The approach

Our research indicated that many people find it difficult to imagine the future even in ten-year increments (Zaidi 2018: 76) and so we opted for a structure that asked small groups to work together to produce snapshots of the world in five-year increments, assembling a linear timeline that would show a plausible progression into the future. To guide them we provided a series of prompts that mixed long-term trends and incremental developments with sudden, sharp shifts. For example:

- The values that suited the old generation are less appealing to a new generation. Why is that? What is changing?

- A major conflict breaks out between two nations or groups whose impacts reverberate throughout society. What is the nature of the conflict? Is it resolved?
- The laws that govern the land grow more restrictive. Where are the greatest interventions being made?
- A natural disaster strikes fear into the heart of the people. How will they prevent it happening in the future?

Once the groups had a single, coherent and plausible timeline they were invited to return to each of the plot nodes they had mapped and sketch out brief 'alternate histories'. This served to destabilize the sense they were producing a single, monolithic vision of the future. The participants found it relatively easy to imagine each of these progressions and in some cases the final snapshot, twenty years in the future, reflected a possibility they hadn't previously considered. In the final exercise they returned to the present state of affairs to brainstorm solutions that could accommodate the potential future trajectories of the world. Our post Story Lab review with the Head of Service for the UNHCR indicated that his most surprising insight came from the separate groups' convergence around the kind of solutions the UNHCR would need to deploy to tackle the breadth of future scenarios. He is now in the early stages of planning pilot projects to leverage those insights and continue collaborations with some of the Lab's participants.

3

Empathize: Imagining extraordinary inner lives

Introduction

'The island of Gont,' writes Ursula K. Le Guin in her most beloved work, *The Wizard of Earthsea*, 'is a land famous for wizards. … Of these some say the greatest, and surely the greatest voyager, was the man called Sparrowhawk, who in his day became both dragonlord and Archmage' (1968: 1). He was the seventh son of a bronze-smith, a goatherd who 'grew wild, a thriving weed, a tall, quick boy, loud and proud and full of temper … always off and away; roaming deep in the forest, swimming in the pools of the River Ar' (ibid.: 2). Yet Sparrowhawk, we learn, was not the wizard's *first* name. That was Duny, the name his mother gifted him before she died.

Names are important in the magical storyworld of Earthsea. Sparrowhawk guards his true name closely for he knows it is a representation of his essence and a dangerous source of power. In fact, the novel's climax hinges upon his own discovery of this name, at which point the fledgling wizard at last comes into his strength as a 'a man: who, knowing his whole true self, cannot be used or possessed by any power other than himself, and whose life therefore is lived for life's sake and never in the service of ruin, or pain, or hatred, or the dark' (ibid.: 180–81). At its heart, then, the novel is an exploration of identity, set against the landscape of a world that crystallizes its importance.

When we follow a character such as Sparrowhawk in a story, we feel things for and with him. We discussed in the previous chapter how a great plot can increase cortisol levels, focusing our attention, but when we add characters into the mix we experience increased oxytocin levels, which affect empathic processes including modulating trust and reducing stress (Stackelberg and McDowell 2015: 63). As Sparrowhawk makes choices and forms relationships with other characters, we learn from these fictional social experiences by simulating his emotions and thoughts (Mar and Oatley 2008). Characters then are both experience simulators (they help us *feel* something about what is happening) and cognitive simulators (they help us *think* about what is happening) as they provide a focal point, helping us navigate the storyworld and creating an emotional connection to the events that unfold.

Some characters are mere observers: they allow us to view events from a certain perspective. Others make things happen. They respond to situations and circumstances, make decisive plans, offer their thoughts, get into fights and generally behave badly. As the author of *The Martian Chronicles* Ray Bradbury offered in his advice to writers,

[find] a character, like yourself, who will want something or not want something, with all his heart. Give him running orders. Shoot him off. Then follow as fast as you can go. The character, in his great love, or hate, will rush you through to the end of the story. The zest and gusto of his need, and there *is* zest in hate as well as in love, will fire the landscape and raise the temperature of your typewriter thirty degrees.

(1992: 7)

Or to reframe it in the advice of game designer John Harper: 'Play your character like you're driving a stolen car' (2017: 202). Characters exist to be used, to test limits and to explore new ideas. The best characters fill us with passionate interest through their very humanity (or indeed inhumanity) and it is this that makes them powerful tools for ideation and communication.

Of course, these characters are not real. They may be based upon research, created as amalgams of data or modelled upon existing people, but fundamentally they are mental constructs – what James N. Frey calls '*homo fictus*' (2010). Yet because well-crafted characters *resemble* people they can help us think about the world in different ways. Even very young children have a surprisingly sophisticated theory of mind – the understanding that other people experience the world differently from them – honed by paying attention and mimicking those around them (Meltzoff 2010). This allows them to judge the intentions of those around them and to better understand their own wants and needs. Invented characters can play a crucial role in this development as children grow older. We shouldn't take this to mean that exploring the minds of others through invented characters is a childish endeavour. On the contrary, humans are hard-wired to use fiction and play to better understand each other's perspectives so we can plan, negotiate and predict how others will behave (Gottschall 2012). As a Story Thinker you can take this skill to a next level, creating convincing characters with believable backstories and selecting the best strategies to put them into play.

This chapter suggests a number of different possible uses for characterization techniques:

- using multiple shallow characters (archetypes, personas) to understand diverse perspectives on a project's use cases or its impacts;

- including hypothetical characters in your scenarios to create deeper engagement and emotional investment in creative teams;

- developing and controlling rounded characters to explore the specific viewpoints, aspects of 'experiential awareness' (Schleicher, Jones and Kachur 2010: 47) and decision-making;

- exploring 'unusual suspects' (Green 2016: 8), people with different backgrounds, histories and experiences who may otherwise be overlooked but who may be recruited as allies for change or represent useful edge cases.

A wide range of fields use characters (in some form) to do this sort of work. For example, Shankar argues that creative writing can connect doctors to 'the world of their patients' (2009: 1604) by helping develop empathy, compassion and critical acumen, a point we pick up in our case study. Likewise, human–computer interaction designers use 'personas' (another way of thinking about characters based on research) to help stakeholders understand their audiences, customers and users (Jansen, Salminen and Jung 2020). Following on this, Fergnani (2019: 446) has adapted the concept of the 'persona' to foresight work to infuse scenarios with life. Many of these approaches borrow directly or obliquely from the field of creative writing. But in centring our understanding in our own disciplinary expertise we provide a practitioner's sense of why these techniques work.

Conceptualizing characterization

Telling details: the whats of character

What defines a character? At the core of most characterization techniques is the understanding that a sense of character arises from the complex interplay of individual traits that comprise anything from their age, background and motivation to whether they are right-handed or left-handed. Samuel R. Delany writes, 'Any two facts clustered around a single pronoun begin to generate a character in the reader's mind' (2013: 77). These traits help a writer grasp the essence of the character's identity. Just as in the previous chapters we have discussed how writers develop a basic premise by asking, 'What if?' and then extrapolate further by asking, 'What else?' so writers follow the same basic principles when creating characters. They start with a few basic traits, sometimes those that pique their interest (say, those that would provide an unusual vantage point into a story or a twist on a well-known trope) or those that are necessary for what the character may need to do in the story (an adventure story may require someone suitable to go on an adventure). Most writers don't know everything about a character upfront. They gradually piece together their understanding, adding or inferring additional traits as they progress.

Just as most storyworlds are deliberately coherent, so too are most characters (Varotsi 2019: 8). This doesn't mean a character can't ever act dissonantly or surprisingly. Often what distinguishes shallow characters from those with greater depth is the sense that not all character traits are obviously linked (some are surprising), making the underlying logic of the character more complicated and less predictable. Real people too have values that conflict with one another, and different situations – even different framings of those situations – can cause them to prioritize one set of values over another. But even the most complex characters should give the impression of *some* unifying sense of who they are, if you want to maintain some level of buy-in (or suspension of disbelief) from your reader.

While depth of character is famously a crucial aspect of literature, you needn't always create the kind of intricate internalization and character development we find in literary novels: your Elizabeth Bennets and Holden Caulfields and Raskolnikovs. Instead, SFF writers, who must balance depth of character against intricacy of plot and scale of world, may focus on characters readers can engage with effectively and efficiently. The author Jeff VanderMeer (2013: 178–81) identifies four main approaches to depth of characterization:

- obsessive-immersive (as close as possible to the interior of the character);

- full or rounded (dipping in and out of the character's interior);

- partial (more limited than full);

- flat or shallow (often archetypal).

These different approaches to character have different uses. An obsessive-immersive approach simulates the richness of another person's emotional experience or the logic of how they think and act in new situations. When translated into a Story Lab, this approach is often best for roleplay activities or writing up scenarios from a specific character's perspective. A shallow character is better suited for rapid perspective-taking activities where participants try to imagine a situation from the viewpoint of multiple characters in succession or to provide a quick access point to a scenario. Many writers start with a shallow character (an archetype, perhaps, such as The Rebel, or a role such as The President of America) and layer in more depth, as necessary.

So how do you give a character depth? Writers tend to focus on concise yet concrete and revealing details about significant characters, and consequently much of this chapter focuses on how to choose these details and put them into play. Providing specific information about a character's interests, appearance, opinions, voice and personal details enhances their realism and allows you to make better decisions about what they might do. James Tiptree Jr exemplifies this approach in the opening paragraph of the short story 'The Only Neat Thing to Do' (1986):

Given one kid, yellow-head, snub-nose-freckles, green-eyes-that-stare-at-you-level, rich-brat, girl-type, fifteen-year old. And all she's dreamed of, since she was old enough to push a hologram button, are heroes of the First Contacts, explorers of the far stars, the great names of Humanity's budding Star Age. She can name you every Discovery Mission; she can sketch you a pretty accurate map of Federation Space and number the Frontier Bases; she can tell you who first contacted every one of the fifty-odd races known; and she knows by heart the last words of Han Lu Han when, himself no more than sixteen, he ran through alien flame-weapons to drag his captain and pilot to safety on Lyrae 91-Beta. She does a little math, too; it's easy for her. And she haunts the spaceport and makes friends with everybody who'll talk to her, and begs rides, and knows the controls of fourteen models of craft. She's a late bloomer, which means the nubbins on her little chest could almost pass for a boy's; and love, great Love, to her is just something pointless that adults do, despite her physical instruction. But she can get into her junior space suit in seventy seconds flat, including safety hooks.

Instantly we know what makes this girl tick: her inner motivations are inseparable from her appearance, relationships, surroundings, behaviour and aspirations. We can already start to predict how she's likely to act as the plot unfolds (she's a bulldog chasing her dreams; come hell or high water, she won't give up; she'll buy her way to the next galaxy if she has to) and what complications might arise to thwart her. This example gives us some starting points about the traits that shape how characters interact with the world: age, gender, socio-economic background, education and physical characteristics are all important.

Shallow characters grow in complexity and nuance as more details accumulate, sometimes through conscious decision-making but just as often through a process of discovery, with a character seeming to act, prompting the writer to develop a rationale for *why* they acted that way after the fact. Ritchie (2017) identifies this as part of a process of negotiating uncertainty in the creative process. Writers often learn more about their characters at the same time as the characters themselves negotiate and discover their own identity. A beautiful example of this is what Kelly Robson (2018) describes as the Luke/Han model of characterization in genre fiction: some characters know what they are trying to do but not who they are (Luke Skywalker on his voyage of self-discovery while he tries to rescue Princess Leia), while others know who they are but not what they want (Han Solo, the rogue smuggler who finally takes on the cause of the Rebellion). This approach demonstrates that a character need not be fully fleshed out to be useful (a common error for new writers who come up with characters so detailed they find it difficult to imagine from their perspectives). Characters are almost always in a state of transition and even as their creator your knowledge will always be partial and subject to revision. This is part of what makes using characters so rewarding: characters can challenge your preconceptions.

Backstory and motivation: the whys of character

It isn't enough to know things *about* your character. Every character needs a *why*, an identity and history that influences their motivations and governs their choices, a sense of the logic that animates who they are. Writers use two elements of character to mobilize otherwise static traits: backstory (where the character has come from) and motivation (what the character wants to do next), and the first always informs the second. Character backstories create verisimilitude and allow a richer exploration of human possibility. It isn't enough to know abstract facts about a character (her favourite colour is yellow, she's a lapsed Catholic who votes to the left). Story Thinkers need to understand the relationship between the character and those facts. Perhaps your character loves yellow because it was the colour her mother always wore to church on Sundays, the only day of the week she seemed happy. Perhaps she is a lapsed Catholic because of the way her mother was convinced by the Church to stay in an abusive marriage. Perhaps she votes to the left because her father was politically conservative and she rejects everything about him. As writers develop a better sense of the *whys* of the character – how all these traits are organically connected – not just the *whats*, they become better able to predict how a character may act in a certain circumstance.

To imagine character backstories, writers often start with a combination of genetic predispositions and environment. A tall white man will almost certainly have a different personal history than a small South Asian woman, who will almost certainly have a different personal history than an interplanetary alien who can shoot poisonous ink out of his fingers. However, if we introduce other starting position factors (perhaps the tall white man was born with a mental illness, perhaps the small South Asian woman was born into extreme wealth, perhaps the alien has such poor motor skills that they are a very poor shot) those differences may defy expectations. Starting traits to consider include race, biological sex and gender, class, embodiedness (e.g. body size, level of ability) and health (both mental and physical), with the recognition that these may change over time. Writers may also imagine different varieties of common human experiences such as their living arrangements, the impact of their relationships, and how they are shaped by the familiar milestones of a life. Where was the character born, where did they grow up, where did they go next? What was their wider environment (economic, social, familial and so on) that these places represented and the events that arose out of that environment?

These facts can then be brought alive by imagining the character in relation to them. Throughout an imagined life, characters will have interacted with many people who may have left a mark on their identity, from an inner circle to an outer circle, with some of those other characters standing as monuments in their lives for good or ill. They will have been shaped, and have feelings about that shaping, by their passages in life: how they have engaged education, work, love and sexuality are all elements of a character's history. If your storyworld is fundamentally different from the real world, then those common elements of a character's history might be quite different. We complement this sketch of a character by imagining the common inner worlds of humans. What are the characters' dreams and aspirations, what do they remember bold and big and what tiny memories glimmer on the edges of their thoughts from time to time? How does this inner life connect to their backstory and why, why, WHY? Never stop asking your characters why.

While much of the above is predicated on imagining common experiences, writers can also make room for imagining uncommon experiences: the startling, wondrous and unpredictable things that are unique to human (and potentially alien or elven or dwarven or … you get the picture) lives. They often include elements of serendipity and coincidence, good and bad fortune, surprises and shocks; and perhaps even things the character has experienced that might have been forgotten such as buried trauma or important things that were overlooked in their lives. These bring a deep understanding of the potential the character represents in the scenario at hand.

Writers use these elements of backstory and motivation to determine a character's likely behaviour, something research in psychology argues humans are good at predicting in the real world. As Thornton and Tamir (2021: 1) argue, social interactions are a complex dance that require us to make accurate predictions about an astonishingly wide array of different actions and activities from concrete physical procedures to abstract social processes, like building consensus. Our predictions are based on a combination of environmental clues about what actions a location allows, perceptual clues that assess a person's physical capabilities and clues about their latent mental state, their goals, intentions and emotions, which are 'excellent predictors of future action' (ibid.). We predict behaviour routinely in the real world with people who are well known to us: most of us know not to antagonize a colleague who is struggling with a deadline and is known for having a short fuse, for example.

Writers take this one step further. They understand that if motivation comprises goals, intentions and emotions, then knowing a character's backstory (past behaviour and social history) can help contextualize and anticipate how they will interact in new situations. If this were laid out as an equation it might look like this:

Given [backstory], if [situation], the character will [X]

There may in fact be many different variations of X, as this is an open-ended rather than a closed equation. Minute changes in the framing of a situation can have large ramifications in human behaviour, particularly in situations of risk, which can make them difficult to predict. As a result, we shouldn't consider character work as necessarily giving a definitive answer. Rather it gives us a range of possibilities.

The kind of situations that are useful to model in this way will be different for different kinds of research projects, ranging from how different people might use a new technology (a common example of how characters are put to use) to how the psychology of a particular person in power might influence the kinds of negotiating strategies that might be effective. In general, though, writers tend to think about situations as being made of some combination of pressure and opportunity. Pressure, as in duress, necessity or antagonistic force (that is, something that forces an action to need to be taken); opportunity, as in the availability and will to act to relieve the pressure (that is, the range of possible choices that could be made). You may have noticed that these are the engines that generate plot, as we discussed in the previous chapter. This reinforces the fact that our four domains are entangled and underscores our point that 'plot driven' and 'character driven' are not particularly useful terms (especially as they are often used to rank creative expression). While Ray Bradbury famously said, 'Plot is no more than footprints left in the snow after your characters have run by on their way to incredible destinations' (1992: 139), it should be noted, too, that what happens in a plot is a significant shaper of character and makes its mark on them: it becomes their new backstory, so to speak, as they make their way through the story.

Strategies for empathizing

In the previous section we outlined approaches to developing characters and determining their trajectory within a story, what they might do when situated within a world and presented with a problem to solve. In this section we present concrete techniques to help you translate these creative writing skills into real-world problem-solving skills. Characterization techniques can be used for perspective-taking, for anchoring convincing and compelling scenarios, or for exploring and anticipating how important decision-makers or actors might behave. As focalizers, characters transform general scenarios into specific stories. In doing so, they draw attention to the fact that the proposed scenarios or use cases are hypothetical: after all, the agents at the heart of them are made-up. Characters, through being wholly imaginary, prove, as it were, that Story Thinking cannot predict the future. This reminder of the hypothetical nature of Story Thinking is useful to help creative collaborators loosen their grip on trying to come up with the 'right' future answer to a problem, and develop more comfort with open-endedness.

However, using characters can feel uncomfortable, particularly for those unpractised in adopting other perspectives. In our own Story Labs, we have noticed participants often instinctively default to well-known archetypes, to characters whose worldview matches their own, or else to famous people that can be easily caricatured. These are all strategies that reduce complexity or lower the chances of social friction (being called out for getting it 'wrong'). These are not bad strategies, per se, but they can mean researchers lose some of the benefits of working with characters.

With those caveats in mind, below we lay out some useful techniques for creating and directing characters.

Roles

It can be useful to begin building a character by thinking about their role, which will often define their place in a story, scenario or situation and their broader objective. For example, in some Story Labs we begin by giving participants characters with simple roles (The Wise Mentor, The Starship Captain, The Journalist and so on), which provides an easy entry point, particularly for participants who may not be used to characterization exercises.

Natures

In cases when a participant may be asked to improvise decisions as a character, we have found it helpful to assign a nature to the character. Of course, characters may have many facets to their nature but choosing a single reference point can help whoever is directing the character to differentiate their own approach to decision-making from that of the character. In roleplaying situations, it also seeds ideas, making it easier for participants to act in new ways and test out approaches because the nature of the character offers them cover. We have included some sample natures below to give a sense of how they work:

- **The Dreamer** – You love grand plans and big ideas.

- **The Peacemaker** – You worry about conflicts and are quick to try to downplay differences.

- **The Moral Compass** – You want to make sure things are done in line with your values, regardless of the outcome.

- **The Adventurer** – You hate inaction and prefer to go out and do something about your problems.

- **The Learner** – You listen carefully to what others say and try to bring together their ideas.

- **The Historian** – You are eager to learn from the past and apply those lessons to present dilemmas.

- **The Optimist** – You are always on the look-out for upsides, even in challenging circumstances.

Objectives, resources, strengths, relationships

When using characters in scenarios, collaborative storytelling, or various kinds of gameplay, you may also assign or give space for participants to develop their own objectives, resources and relationships. Objectives work best if they are straightforward ('Lead your band to the castle!') but also give room for participants to determine the best strategies for meeting the objectives. Resources or strengths may give some indication of what those best strategies are. Assigning relationships with other characters can encourage participants to interact with each other.

Character questionnaires

Writers often use 'twenty questions' style character questionnaires to flesh out characters quickly. Answering these questions from a character's perspective not only elicits facts about their backstory, some of which are unexpected, but also prompts reflection on the character's relationship to those facts. This allows you to build-up your sense of the logic of the character so you can better predict their behaviour. We provide a sample in Chapter 7.

Using research

Research can help make characters more realistic. Strategies might include:

- interviews, surveys and focus groups;
- 'big data' sets;
- secondary literature and 'grey' literature;
- anecdotal research (e.g. speaking with friends and colleagues) and autoethnographies;
- engaging sensitivity readers;

- field work, site visits, bodystorming and other forms of experiential research.

Writers typically use interviews, anecdotal research, field work and sensitivity readers, that is, cultural experts who can shed light on alternative perspectives that may be misrepresented. The use of sensitivity readers, in particular, reflects Nisi Shawl's point that 'cultural background is data. If you want it, and you don't have it, it's valuable; treat it that way' (Shawl 2009).

Most researchers have traditionally used qualitative data sets to develop personas but as data collection tools are refined and quantitative data becomes more readily accessible, some fields such as human–computer interaction are already seeing new strategies for the rapid and responsive development of personas through algorithms (Jansen, Salminen and Jung 2020). Quantitative research may be effective in helping you decide which traits to attach to your characters but if you want to humanize the data (Friess 2012), we recommend experimenting with qualitative and experiential forms of research. These will help you get a better feel for putting that character in a situation.

Thinking in character

A range of approaches can help participants think 'in character', including anything from light roleplaying (answering a questionnaire in the first person, pretending to be the character) to more sustained roleplay (creating a character and making decisions as that character for several activities, perhaps even incorporating props) to journalling (writing down the thoughts of the character). We find it is helpful to begin with a few key ideas about a character, perhaps their role, their nature and a few character traits or elements of backstory, and then place them in a situation. The more you spend time imagining life as that character or practise making decisions as that character, the more you will come to flesh out other elements of their life or discover facts about them that help you make sense of how all disparate parts of the character fit together. If this feels difficult, remember these are skills writers practise regularly. When we work on novels, we will sometimes spend months or even years thinking about characters, imagining them in new situations and working out their relationships to other characters. This is one of the most enjoyable aspects of the writing process.

Challenges

Characters can be incredibly rewarding because they offer new perspectives and force you to consider new possibilities. But characterization can take some time to master. Below we list some common mistakes:

- incoherent characters possessing too many disparate traits;

- unrealistic characters that bear no relationship to research;

- overdetermined characters created to represent a particular viewpoint or justify a use case;

- characters too shallow to offer genuine insights;

- characters too complicated to use practically because they take too long to understand or master;

- stereotypical characters, when depth is required;

- homogeneous characters that match the character creator and don't give fresh perspectives.

The last point is particularly important. Character work can be uncomfortable. The notion that one has to write authentically has sometimes been misconceived as a directive to stick strictly to one's own lane and avoid exploring perspectives beyond personal familiarity. This view does a disservice to the potential of creative writing. Sensitively and intentionally engaging in creative writing opens up the ability to imagine and empathize with different viewpoints. There are insights about research projects (your fellow researchers, your immediate end-users, those who might be affected by your research or who might have an impact on it) which can be gleaned through perspective-taking techniques but the greater the distance from your own viewpoint and that of the viewpoint you are investigating, the more conscious work you will have to do to generate useful insights. A better approach is to embrace the principle of 'Write what you know – and if you don't know, find out.' This encourages you to actively seek knowledge, conduct research and engage with diverse perspectives.

Shawl and Ward (2005) argue there are particular traits that indicate 'marked difference' which may need to be handled with additional sensitivity: race, orientation, ability, age, religion, sex and class. Some of these traits, age and sex, for example, are likely to be part of your basic building blocks and so it is difficult to get away with avoiding them. In fact, explicitly avoiding them doesn't solve the problem: when we don't consciously make decisions we tend to default to traits which ultimately either resemble ourselves or resemble cultural stereotypes. But working with characters is a skillset that you can improve. One of the key ways you can do this is through reflection. These questions can help you to guide and refine your activities:

- *Noticing embedded assumptions*: Are there character behaviours or perspectives that seem to naturally flow from one or more of the traits you are examining? What makes these seem natural? What kinds of assumptions have you made and what is the source of those assumptions? What sorts of research would help you put pressure on or support your assumptions?

- *Avoiding stereotypes*: Are there sets of traits you have picked that seem like a natural group? What makes these seem natural? What happens when one of these traits is switched out for another, particularly one of the marked traits we discussed above?

- *Exploring the edges*: Have you only chosen dominant traits? Are there edge cases which might reveal unexpected or overlooked perspectives, what Duncan Green calls 'unusual suspects' (2016: 8)? Examples include community insiders who could make a difference but may not necessarily be the people usually thought of as changemakers or power brokers, disempowered people who experience the worst aspects of decisions made at the centre of government, or people at the middle of a chain of bureaucracy who may observe much but have little influence over what they see.

If you have already filled out a character questionnaire, it can be revealing to go back and make conscious decisions to flip some of the traits you may have unconsciously determined. It's important to remember that these identity traits don't inherently determine or predict anything about an individual or their behaviour. So where does that leave you? Firstly, it suggests that character work is not predictive nor should it replace genuine engagement or collaboration with those who have a stake in your research. Secondly, just because identity traits can't predict behaviours with certainty doesn't mean that research can't be useful for you. This work may provide:

- a deeper understanding of dominant identities, beliefs and behaviours common to a group you are interested in learning more about;

- a rich variety of differences in identities, beliefs and behaviours within that same group;

- an awareness of alternative systems of understanding the world, different operational realities and their importance.

These insights can help inform your work simply by disrupting expectations and assumptions and revealing places where you may need to dig deeper, do more research, or engage in consultation.

Although an awareness of difference is good, it can also be productive to focus on how cultural and social histories might frame similarities. Science fiction writer Lavie Tidhar observes that 'human nature itself hasn't changed a great deal' over time, even though individual people or broader societies can radically change relatively quickly (2022). Likewise, Ellen Kushner and Delia Sherman emphasize the 'emotional constants that connect us', including our human responses to death, parenthood, homesickness, fear and so on (2022). The point is that everybody is finding a way to cope with these human disturbances and joys – everybody has the same things that they do differently (Kushner and Sherman 2022). No matter how strange or different people may seem, there remains a touchstone human element, that human connection. Being human is being human (Tidhar 2022). Even if you put diverse characters against the most dazzling future, you're still telling the same human story (Tidhar 2022; Kushner and Sherman 2022).

Conclusion

In this chapter we've explored some of the ways fictional characters function in stories. As focal points in the grand scheme of things, they narrow general events down to personal and specific perspectives, acting as our guides and emotional touchstones throughout the narrative. Often, they're catalysts whose aspirations and actions propel the plot forward, but they can also be invested bystanders – Nick Carraway in *The Great Gatsby* by F. Scott Fitzgerald (1950), for example, caught up in the whirlwind of Gatsby's extravagant lifestyle – whose positions in the imagined world directly influence how readers experience it. Characters can be 'flat' or 'shallow' figures (like archetypes and stereotypes) built more for instant recognition than originality; they can also be 'rounded' individuals, whose familiar motivations, desires and behaviours engage and sustain our interest. Beyond that, they can also embody subject positions, histories and realities far beyond any we've ever known ourselves. In effectively dislodging us from our comfort zones, these 'unusual suspects' remind us that – despite many possible points of connection – the human experience is not always universal. Whether they're heroes, villains or supporting actors whose narrative paths briefly intersect with our guide's, characters are intentionally crafted to make us think and feel while reading – in other words, to empathize – and to reflect on these thoughts and feelings long after we've turned the last page.

We've also suggested techniques for creating realistic, convincing, believable characters – give them detailed backstories, unique quirks and appearances and interests, distinct wants and whys – but we'd like to take a moment now to note the incredible power of the unbelievable in storytelling. When it comes to characterization, SFF stories offer what no other genre can: the chance to take people and our problems out of this world. To imagine fully realized, complex, compelling beings who aren't constrained by humanity's social, historical, cultural or physical baggage. To let distance and difference shed new, bright light on the darkest of our Earthly matters. To think beyond patriarchal orders, gender binaries, capitalist systems, biological imperatives and other forces humans have constructed, wielded and weaponized for centuries to govern, constrain, oppress and/or threaten our lives on this planet – and instead to consider other (hopefully better) ways of existing together.

THE WORST DAY OF YOUR LIFE: A CASE STUDY IN DEVELOPING SOFT SKILLS IN MEDICAL STUDENTS

The project

Creative Writing for Clinical Excellence (hereafter, CWCE) was a thirteen-week elective that ran for two years in the University of Queensland's Doctor of Medicine programme. Our stated aim in developing CWCE was to allow students to develop necessarily 'soft skills', as opposed to the 'hard' science skills medical students are preoccupied with in their studies. While introducing creative writing to medical curricula is not new (Cowen, Kaufman and Schoenherr 2016), the extent and depth of this training was enhanced by its length and by the fact it was taught by practising creative writers, two of whom had studied medicine before turning to creative writing (and one of whom is a science fiction writer). The creative writing skills developed were grounded in repeated practice, rather than touched on lightly and hypothetically. The course tended towards a final full-length written piece of work aimed to bed down key learnings so that they might stay with the emerging medical practitioners throughout their careers.

The challenge

The problem the course aimed to solve was an acknowledged lack of soft skills in practising medical professionals. Rana Awdish's 2018 book *In Shock* is critical of medical training that produces doctors who are blunt and indifferent at best, or coolly hostile at worst. By contrast, Mark Wilson (2018) outlines the important therapeutic impact of a good bedside manner, citing studies that show it leads to better outcomes for patients with hypertension or breast cancer. While medical school curricula are outstanding at teaching medical knowledge, the ongoing challenge is teaching 'soft skills in critical thinking, listening and verbal expression' which are vital for good communication with patients and therefore more accurate diagnoses and effective treatment (Cowen, Kaufman and Schoenherr 2016: 311).

Creative writing instruction has been widely offered to doctors-in-training as part of soft skills training, but a literature review by Cowen, Kaufman and Schoenherr (2016) showed that the largest proportion of the creative work emerging doctors were asked to produce was reflective and self-expressive, seen as keys to enhance compassion. CWCE's more specific intervention was allowing students to take the perspective of patients – what they might reflect on or how they might express themselves – by imagining their internal worlds.

The approach

CWCE featured multiple touchpoints to understanding empathy and perspective-taking, including three two-hour dedicated seminars about techniques for imagining characters from the inside. Activities included adding nuance to stereotypes, upending assumptions about characters' behaviour, understanding an imaginary world through characters' senses, and imagining the relationships between characters and their preferences and worldviews. The final creative piece that participants worked towards over the thirteen weeks was to rewrite a clinical case from the patient's perspective:

> Write a short story that re-imagines a real case from the patient's point-of-view. You are free to select a [de-identified] case you have seen yourself in clinical practice … The short story may imagine any aspect of the patient's life and experiences in connection with their medical experience. The objective is to reorient the perspective of the story from doctor to patient.

Positive feedback from evaluations at the end of the CWCE opportunity helps to put the value of this into context. As one student noted, medical practitioners are often trying to solve a science problem while patients are 'having the most vulnerable times of their life'. They go on to write that learning fiction techniques taught them about 'occupying someone else's identity and exploring how they would feel and react under different circumstances. I think that we have all visited doctors who might have found that helpful.' Participants noted not only how developing these skills might help future patients directly, but also indirectly through improving the participants' sense of well-being. One loosened their grip on their perfectionism: 'over the last few months I've discovered that it's actually fine to be writing things that are imperfect'; another was able to transfer the skills beyond the course: 'Imagining creative solutions for these characters has encouraged me to be more creative in finding solutions to difficulties arising in my own life.' But, most importantly, many found the act of playing with their new imaginary friends an opportunity to 'breathe and rediscover some of the things that make life beautiful'. As one respondent noted, 'In a career with such high rates of burnout, finding outlets is extremely important not just for our own mental health but to ensure that patient care is of the highest standard'.

4

Engage: The magic words that build connection and understanding

Introduction

The longhouse is shorter than its name implies. Thirty paces from end to end, if we're being generous; more like twenty for Magnus, the tallest warrior, swaying over a hornful of his lord's strongest brew, a bowl of stew scraped clean on the trestle before him. His belly roils as the hall pitches, unmoored on an ale-tossed sea. Skål, he roars with the other men, dousing his beard with foam. The hearth blazes nearby, sucking air from the room, belching smoke. It murks the gabled ceiling, blurs timber walls and pillars, shrouds the bloodied crew celebrating beneath raven-stamped banners.

Magnus blinks, head heavy as an ox, plodding deeper and deeper into a furrow of mud. He's only a few gulps away from oblivion now, so let's intervene: what say we crack open the hall's great oaken doors, invite in the hooded poet skulking out there, and let the winter's coldest talons shear through the fug to grip Magnus's blond braids and yank his thick skull up off the table. 'Hwæt!'

booms the poet – a *scop* in this context, an Old English orator, hired to flatter, entertain and commemorate heroes. Like the *Beowulf* poet, whose famous first word is the subject of decades of debate, he seizes attention with his alliterative verse, his vivid vocabulary, his fabulous style.

While the reader of a story may be curious about a storyworld, hooked by a plot, or fascinated by a character, all this work is done in and through language. This echoes a provocative point M. John Harrison made about his seminal fantasy world Viriconium: that it is not a real place; rather, it is 'just some words' (2001). For Harrison, language is generative, exciting the imagination because of its inherent unreliability: 'Language is a scandal because – by an abuse of its own basic assumption, which is that it has some honest marriage with the real – it can make connections. ... Words pass the experienced world back and forth between them as a metaphor of a metaphor, the sign of a sign' (Harrison 1989: 13). While Harrison is most interested in the moment at which language becomes exhausted and meaning breaks down, we ourselves move in the opposite direction. We find the simultaneous slipperiness and specificity of language energizes our practice because it prompts us to consider what we are saying, what it might mean to a reader and what it might signal about the story. This leads to the theme of this chapter, that language creates possibilities, aids extrapolation and needs to be calibrated. Language has been recognized, even mythologized, as a powerful force for centuries in Western thought. Renaissance magicians such as Edmund Spenser's Merlin in *The Faerie Queene* can 'by words ... call out of the sky/Both Sunne and Moone, and make them him obay' (1978: 3.12.1–2); more recently, scholars have recognized the importance of inclusive language in fostering diversity and equity across society. It would be a short-sighted Story Thinker who overlooked the richness that words bring to making sense of complex problems.

This chapter brings a particular focus to the importance of style, tone and figurative language. In our opening description, our sentences alternate between the short and sharp and the long and languid. Similes create strong sensory experiences – the belly that roils like a sea – while active verbs – the hearth blazing, sucking air, belching smoke – immerse the reader in the setting and infuse the prose with energy. *Skål* is left untranslated: it gives a sense of colour and authenticity while inviting the reader to look closely at the context for meaning. Writers deploy all these tools of linguistic craft to create precise effects. Some activities aligned with this domain include:

- inviting audiences into a story, experience or activity, capturing their attention and setting expectations;

- creating a rapport and building trust between collaborators;

- using evocative details to provoke the imagination;

- deploying figurative language to apprehend nuances, cross disciplinary divides and reduce 'instrumentalized, mechanistic thinking' (Sicart 2014: 5);

- wielding metaphors to produce powerful new understandings and share knowledge;

- understanding techniques for creating closure, inviting reflection and meaning-making.

While plot, setting and character are the building blocks of story, they are enriched and amplified by carefully deployed language and style.

Conceptualizing style and language

The invitation to the reader

Every story must invite the reader (or viewer or collaborator) in and set their expectations. Writers use textual elements such as word choice, grammar and even sentence or paragraph length as well as broader paratextual elements such as book covers, author endorsements, blurbs and the like. This resonates with what Finn and Wylie call the 'aesthetics' of the invitation (2021), a term borrowed from theatre studies to conceptualize the way that an audience can be positioned to participate in the story or, in their examples, event. It encompasses 'the typical event logistics of work sites and catering, but also the way in which the project is described, the affective tone of communications, the design of collateral and workshop materials, and all other aspects of the project' (ibid.: 7). A good invitation sets expectations and creates social glue.

In the scene above, what work does the word *hwæt* do? In the storyworld, it signals the *scop* is about to begin, but in the broader framing, it welcomes the reader into the warriors' raucous hall (conceptually immersing them as we discussed in Chapter 1) while also creating a frisson through its strangeness. Here we can see how language can be deeply contextual with respect to a place, person or situation. While contemporary readers may find the word unfamiliar, for the poet *hwæt* is undoubtedly the best word, appropriate to both his character and setting, natural in his voice. It's a verbal palm-slap on the table. 'Listen up, folks,' he is telling his brethren in the longhouse, 'I've got a story to tell you!'

Words also have historical and cultural dimensions which shape how we understand them. Here, *hwæt* echoes the first line of *Beowulf*, that most epic of Old English poems. Of course, we could have translated the word in a variety of ways, each with their own subtle inflection. We could have created a deeper sense of gravity by following the tradition of nineteenth- and twentieth-century scholars who substituted it with words like 'Lo!', 'Behold!' 'Aye!' and 'Listen!' Maria Dahvana Headley kicked off her 2020 interpretation of *Beowulf* with 'Bro!' (2021: 3). Irreverent, even a little risky, this laddish colloquialism invites a new relationship to the work. This isn't some dusty old book with no relevance for the modern world, she implies – here is a story about boasting, violence and the nature of masculinity that could tell us as much about the workings of a football team as it does about Anglo-Saxon warriors. In this way, the considered choice of words can shape audience expectations and create powerful connections between discrete ideas or contexts.

Voice, tone and register

As we have hinted, writers must choose the right language and voice to communicate concepts and content. This requires them to think deeply about their audiences. How experienced are the readers? How young or old? How familiar are they with the genre or subject matter? How much time and energy are they willing (or able) to spend with this story? And, significantly, how will the style help them to enjoy, reflect upon and value this experience? The choice of words, and their arrangement for style and syntax, can add rich layers to a story experience.

Some of the main ways writers do this are through voice, tone and register. Elements of voice often refer to a writer's personality, identity and worldview. Often writers approach 'finding their voice' as a pseudo-mystical process but this, we suspect, speaks to the power and confidence that comes with finding an authentic style for communication. More focus is placed on voice in literary contexts but it crops up in academic ones as well. Potgieter and Smit characterize voice as 'our scholarly identity in our craft', which involves finding 'knowledge and understanding that is blended into our identity' (2009: 215–16). The problem is that, as Leo Hamalian points out, much bad academic prose 'sounds as though it had been ground out by a sausage machine or produced with labor pains' (1970: 227). An authentic voice, however, allows you to speak naturally with authority.

Tone connects writer and reader more closely, indicating an attitude toward the subject and inviting the reader to share it. It should be no surprise that the words 'tone' and 'tune' are related etymologically; like music, tone is something people listen for to guide their expectations and it helps people attune with each other. For example, in science fiction it's a common challenge to introduce futuristic realities and/or complex scientific concepts in a way that readers aren't bombarded with new ideas in a dense or impenetrable tone. We want to immerse them into this strange new world rather than block them out with a thick wall of text. Like Andy Weir in his bestselling 2014 novel *The Martian*, we might opt for straightforward prose laced with black humour:

LOG ENTRY: SOL 6

I'm pretty much screwed.

That's my considered opinion.

Screwed.

Six days into what should be the greatest month of my life, and it's turned into a nightmare.

I don't even know who'll read this. I guess someone will find it eventually. Maybe a hundred years from now.

(2014: 1)

Although many readers will remember *The Martian* for its plot, it is Mark Watney's engaging, familiar tone (the voice of his character, yes, but also the novel's broader approach to its subject) that transforms scientific jargon and pages-long info-dumping about how to survive on Mars into a memorable and fast-paced adventure.

Register refers to more specific elements of word choice and grammar, sliding from informal to formal. For example, if our aim in telling a story is to entertain a young person, then perhaps we might choose a reassuring, omniscient narrator, as J. R. R. Tolkien does in *The Hobbit*: 'This of course is the way to talk to dragons, if you don't want to reveal your proper name (which is wise), and don't want to infuriate them by a flat refusal (which is also very wise). No dragon can resist the fascination of riddling talk and of wasting time trying to understand it' (2013: 275). Part of the delight of reading this novel is the shift in register that comes from being directly addressed in moments of tension like this one. Here we find Bilbo – a small creature who's very fond of the comforts of home, and with whom many readers (young and old) can therefore identify – overcoming his fears, sneaking into the dragon's lair and riddling dangerously with him. The register reassures Tolkien's audience, in this case children, that they are safe in his authorial hands. We talk about specific features of psychological comfort and safety within creative environments in Chapter 5, but it is worth noting here that many readers are more likely to tackle challenging material if the author deliberately builds a rapport.

Voice tends to be consistent across a story, but both tone and register can change. For example, the earthy and whimsical chapters in Hobbiton in Tolkien's *Fellowship of the Ring* contrast with the heavier and indeed more dramatic passages describing the forging of the fellowship later in the novel. Switches such as these can jolt readers awake, change the mood, provide contrast and interest, and intensify different emotions. Tone and register are also most noticeable when they are inconsistent or incongruent: old-fashioned, mildly sexist jokes with a contemporary audience, or sweary comments at a church fete, for example. There is no more effective lesson on the value of tone than reading a romance novel of mostly nineteenth-century manners, which is latterly interrupted by an erotic scene where our hero works his heroine like a piece of farm machinery. It has happened to us. We know.

One final element of tone worth considering is the function of estrangement or defamiliarization. Defamiliarization is a literary concept that originated with Russian Formalist theorists, particularly Viktor Shklovskij, in the early twentieth century (1998). It involves presenting ordinary objects, situations or words in a way that makes them seem strange (the opposite of *The Martian*, which takes a strange situation and uses tone to normalize it). The purpose of defamiliarization is to encourage readers to break free of habituated patterns of thought. It does this by heightening perception, prompting readers to notice details and nuances they might otherwise have overlooked, and encouraging reflection on how to make sense of what they have observed. Darko Suvin, whom we discussed in Chapter 1, applied the concept specifically to science fiction. He argues when SFF stories with their non-realistic elements are told in a matter-of-fact or realistic manner, we feel cognitively estranged from our conventional understanding of reality. The resulting psychological distance allows us to think about the world (the storyworld and the real world) and its underpinning logic in new ways ([1979] 2016).

Sparking the imagination and making meaning

Wolfgang Iser, the father of the reader reception movement, was very clear that stories are experiences, not static objects, and that readers are actively engaged by reading, not passive consumers (1980). Green and Brock call the effect of storytelling on the imagination 'transportation', which they describe as 'a distinct mental process, an integrated melding of attention, imagery, and feelings' (2000: 701). A transported reader, as the term indicates, becomes focused on the storyworld and loses connection to or focus on the 'world of origin' (ibid.: 702). In this state, transported readers 'may experience strong emotions and motivations' related to their individual beliefs and attitudes (ibid.: 702). Engagement through imagination, then, leads to investment because imagination is personal.

This kind of engagement happens at the level of words, which create strong mental images. Upon reading the line, 'She had long red hair', the typical reader's imagination fires up and creates an image. The more detailed the line – 'Her hair hung in loose curls to her waist, a pale ginger like the moon above a forest fire' – the more likely the image is to stick in the reader's imagination. The words we choose imbue elements of the world with attributes that allow us to not only imagine them more vividly – but also to imagine other possibilities for how they might be.

Figurative language can do this work particularly well because it grants writers opportunities for ambiguity, novelty and meaning-making. The overarching term figurative language refers to similes (your smile is like a rose), metaphors (my heart is a paper boat on a calm lake), personification (the clock ticked watchfully) or any other non-literal phrases or ideas that we use to talk about one thing by comparing it to something else. This kind of language, the language of poetry, is 'both attention-seeking and attention-rewarding' (Jones 2012: 1). If in conversation with a male colleague, we took the time to describe the pain of childbirth as though a great cast-iron, steam-powered machine has possessed your body and suddenly been thrown into a thunderous reverse, its gears clanking and grinding against the other, our colleague would come closer to understanding than if we just said, 'It hurts a lot.' (It has happened to us. We know.) More than that, the time we had spent elaborating the image would have invited him to pay attention, jolting him out of any minimizing habituated thoughts he might have had about the experience. Language like this also comes in handy when one person doesn't have access to another's experience or when language is limited in one area but more robust in another (in English we have more words to describe sight than we do taste, for example). This is why the way we talk about abstract ideas is often suffused with figurative language, not simply because this language can be beautiful (though it often is) but because it allows us to apprehend complexity and create analogies.

In SFF stories, metaphors serve as powerful tools of conceptual framing, organization and compression. They act as narrative lenses through which complex or abstract ideas can be presented in a more understandable and relatable manner. Through metaphorical comparisons, authors can frame the conceptual landscape of their imaginative worlds, guiding readers in how they should perceive and interpret the story's unique elements. For example, N. K. Jemisin's *Broken Earth* series of fantasy novels (2015–17) can be read as a metaphor for institutionalized racism in the United States, while Ursula K. Le Guin's short story *The Ones Who Walk Away from Omelas* is a piercing extended metaphor about the moral failings of global capitalism. These metaphors compress multifaceted ideas and speculative concepts into concise forms that allow readers to consider them in new ways.

The aesthetics of the exit

We wrote earlier about the aesthetics of the invitation, a theory borrowed from drama and repurposed for scenario planning and futures thinking. Here, we want to advance some ideas about the aesthetics of the exit. The underpinning creative writing theory we bring to this is as follows: stories don't just peter out, or at least the good ones don't. Writers take the time to craft an ending, so that the reader leaves with a strong impression that both satisfies and lingers in the mind. How a novel ends matters because it has a profound impact on the reader's emotional and intellectual engagement with the story, organizing their overall reading experience. A well-crafted ending can elevate a novel from a mere sequence of events to a meaningful and memorable narrative.

There is a range of story-ending techniques. In some genres, such as mysteries and thrillers, writers often use twist endings where they reveal surprising information or a hidden truth that redefines the entire narrative. A tie-back ending will point back to a hint on the first page, giving a feeling of circularity. Open-ended endings hint or gesture somewhere else as a way to spark imagination and curiosity in the reader. A happy ending can be uplifting. An ambiguous ending can be mysterious and invite further reflection about the nature of the story and its elements. An epilogue can provide a snapshot of the characters far in the future, shifting perspectives and reframing the conclusion. Ultimately, the conclusion of a story plays a crucial role in shaping our interpretation by offering closure, impacting our emotions and influencing our sense of meaning. It underscores the ending's significance in shaping our cognitive and emotional responses.

Strategies for engaging

Why does language matter for real-world problem solving? Well, most of the complex problems that researchers and thinkers might grapple with don't exist in one discipline. Marlies Whitehouse and team argue that language awareness, comprehensibility, context awareness, professional setting and transdisciplinarity – which they define as 'research on, for, and with practitioners' who are 'experts in the research process' and who work 'across and beyond academic and non-academic disciplines and fields' (2021: 6) – are fundamental to collaborative problem solving. Like us, they believe that a 'mutually understandable, common language is a pivotal tool to negotiate the framework and conditions of such multilayered collaboration, but also to sustainably solve the targeted problems together' (ibid.: 12). In their science-based, ethnographic approach to strategic communication across knowledge specializations, McGreavy et al. demonstrate that 'a focus on definitions, audience, and expertise can produce knowledge about some of the complex and multidimensional ways that strategic communication shapes collaboration' (2022: 10). Their research 'centers a strategy of continuously posing questions' (ibid.) that considers audience interests and varying levels of expertise, tactically avoids or employs discipline-specific jargon, and hopes to 'transform inequitable communication patterns' (ibid.: 1). These scholars give us a sense of some of the key points of crossover in language use.

Metaphors are also important here. In her landmark book on interdisciplinarity, Julie Klein posits there is something fundamentally metaphorical about the way that teams who span disciplines may share concepts and models: 'Borrowing is metaphoric in several ways. Theories and models from other disciplines may sensitize scholars to questions not usually asked in their own fields, or they may help interpret and explain, whether that means a framework for integrating diverse elements or hypothetical answers that cannot be obtained from existing disciplinary resources' (1990: 93). A metaphor, like a borrowed conceptual tool, may 'function as a probe, facilitating understanding and enlightenment. Or, it may provide insight into another system of observational categories and meanings, juxtaposing the familiar with the unfamiliar' (ibid.). Finding this common ground may create social cohesion. Writers are attuned to the ways that figurative language can function to bond people in not only a practical sense (through creating a shared language that transcends disciplines) but also in an affective sense (by creating cohorts with their own set of in-jokes and cultural references), on which we will write more in Chapter 6.

With this in mind, below we outline some key strategies for engaging creative problem-solving teams, establishing rapport and creating meaning.

Inviting the reader in

One way we begin is by calibrating Story Thinkers' expectations before anyone attends a Lab. First and foremost, we want them to know that our time together will be lively, inventive, inspiring. As this book no doubt makes clear, using boring language is anathema to creative writers like us. Being professional and authoritative in any form of communication shouldn't preclude being captivating, so our first *hwæt!* to catch Story Thinkers' attention – and to foreshadow the style of our Lab – takes place in the invitation to participate. Our invitations might ask provocative questions or else give a taste of the world or scenario the Lab might explore. Story Thinking sessions are not black-tie affairs, so our emails are pitched accordingly. These friendly emails tend to avoid honorifics, but our conversational tone is nevertheless respectful.

Choosing your tone

Think about the kind of experience you want to create and the kind of audience you have, then choose the tone to match. We wouldn't recommend anything too formal for creative activities. If you want the unexpected to arise, then it's a good idea to set that tone with words and ideas that are unexpected. A key weapon in the arsenal of tone is humour, especially when engaging people in a creative activity. Being open about your own limitations, encouraging others to make light of their own and creating opportunities for play and fun are all ways to generate a tone where humour can thrive. When it does, through in-jokes and call-backs related to the material, participants will bond and remember the lessons learned more readily.

Varying your tone

An awareness of tonal variations can help you control the emotional journey your participants go on. For example, in the typical introduction to a workshop we may begin by acknowledging the Traditional Owners of the land on which we are meeting and ask for a moment of reflection, then introduce ourselves and establish our credibility as presenters, often by citing our accomplishments, before outing ourselves as geeks as a way to shift the tone, show a little vulnerability and create a rapport. Each of these 'moves' involves a change in approach that often manifests in the language we adopt, our use of slides and even our body language. In some cases, we may go further than this by choosing explicit points to drop out of the role of instructor or facilitator and into the role of storyteller by purposefully using heightened language to momentarily take on the role of a character, introduce a story setting or narrate a particular plot point or crisis.

Addressing the imagination in simple ways

A shortcut to engaging the imagination is to be specific and personal. If you are co-creating a future version of the town you're in, for example, anchoring that imagining with evocative, specific images that relate to people will connect with your participants very quickly. Yes, you can talk about a town surrounded by red dust and heat haze; but if you describe the way the dust gets in your mouth on blustery days, or the way the heat sizzles bare feet on the crackling grass … you can drop your participant into the world quickly.

A key lesson here is using the senses to describe things. The visual is important, but there are (at least) four other senses: smell, taste, touch/feel and sound. For those who want to range a little further, you can explore the sense of how time passes (chronoception), how the body is positioned in space (proprioception), or how we balance ourselves and stay upright (equilibrioception). While these may not seem like obvious points of reference for most settings, they may well come into play in unusual environments (aboard a ship or other vehicle – or even on another planet). Depending on who you read, there are others, though unfortunately we lack the electromagnetic sense that helps sharks find their prey in water. Be careful out there!

Using metaphors to develop shared understanding

If a team chooses and extends a metaphor, they can use it to create a shared language. A researcher on family law may talk about divorce as being like some kind of dramatic incident, for example a shipwreck. There's stormy weather for a long time and then everything falls apart. So what aspect of family law and policy might others from different disciplines bring this to approach? Perhaps it could help them think about resilience for families after divorce: getting on the lifeboat early and getting away from the wreck before it drags everyone under. Maybe it could help them think through financial arrangements: knowing where the treasure chest is if you need to leave a sinking ship in a hurry. Maybe it could shed light on the emotional complexities of repartnering: how do we practise self-care when we get to shore? That metaphor can be a touchstone for talking about a shared problem and a way to get back on the same page when team members feel they are missing each other.

If you are working with a team who repeatedly uses a metaphor or a set of other figurative ideas, it's always a good idea to make some time to unpack them. One group we worked with likened their project to a merry-go-round, and it was through talking out that metaphor that their frustration at the same problems arising again and again was expressed. We then used the metaphor to think about what they wanted: to be enchanted so they could become free horses, galloping over the horizon into the new ground they knew their research could find. It allowed us to talk about what kind of energy in the real world could perform that enchantment: what allies they could make, what policies they could influence and so on; and from there what kind of practical steps they could take to remove their fixings and enact that change. This can also be a good way to make sense of implausible suggestions: by treating them as metaphors.

Finding ways to say what cannot or should not be said

Story Thinking can be, in itself, figurative: using story to talk about things that are difficult to talk about directly because they are too emotionally charged or, in some cases, because they may contain information that should not be shared widely (perhaps it contains personal details or in the cases of military audiences it may be classified). SFF stories have historically served as powerful and often subversive forms for offering societal critiques that might be challenging to voice openly due to political or social constraints, resistance or censorship.

Finding the right name

Sometimes finding the right word for an object, character or idea can give it additional weight or resonance. Consider William Gibson's use of the word 'cyberspace' which we discussed in Chapter 1. The word concretized the concept because it was both evocative and memorable. Likewise we began Chapter 3 with a discussion of Ursula K. Le Guin's character Sparrowhawk and the power of naming.

Ending well

Story Labs can be intense experiences and we have found it useful to think about the particular exercises or conclusions we use in order to provide a sense of resolution. We've used variations of the four following approaches:

- **Summarizing the experience**: We often ask participants to write down a thought or phrase that names the feeling they are leaving with. This is intended for them and them alone, and does not necessarily need to be shared. This exercise can be particularly effective after potentially emotional exercises because it gives a structured space for quiet, independent reflection.

- **Reflecting on lessons learned**: We tend to reserve the last fifteen minutes (or longer) of a workshop for participants to offer their own reflections on what they will take away from the workshop. This allows them to articulate what they have found valuable, and it also prompts others in the room to hear those responses.

- **Using a cliffhanger**: For workshops embedded in a sequence or in a broader programme of research, consider highlighting what aspects of the question haven't been resolved or need further consideration. These final 'hooks' can provide a prompt that encourages participants to continue to engage with each other on the problem and can spark interest in what comes next.

- **Finding a higher register**: For Story Labs that deal with sensitive or emotional subjects it can be useful to find a way to shift the register in the conclusion. For instance, in our workshop with the UNHCR (discussed in Chapter 2) we chose to conclude with an excerpt of 'Home Poem' by Warsan Shire, a British writer, poet, editor and teacher, who was born to Somali parents in Kenya. This provided a shared emotional moment that re-centred the workshop on the human dimensions of humanitarian crises.

Challenges

While writers have the luxury of time (comparatively, given we are always feeling pressed about deadlines), it can be difficult to curate and deploy language intentionally and effectively when improvising in a Story Lab. The best language for such an occasion may be that which is simple and fits the tone. Likewise, you probably don't want to reach too far for chimerical words and phantasmagorical metaphors (see what we did there?) if you are working with a team of engineers whose first language isn't English. Some other common challenges include:

- creating the wrong first impression, either by being too serious when playfulness is required or being too playful when you need to establish credibility;

- ill-timed or tone-deaf jokes;

- DNA (do not abbreviate) (Barnett and Doubleday 2020);

- choosing gendered language that risks alienating collaborators or making them uncomfortable;

- failing to translate words or concepts that may be specific to a discipline (your own included), thereby excluding some collaborators;

- failing to slow down sufficiently, unpack colloquialisms or speak plainly when working with collaborators for whom English is not a first language;

- letting an activity peter out without a strong resolution, typically because you or your collaborators are too tired at the end of the day.

It is everyone's job to choose their language carefully and to monitor and guide the language of others. But if you find yourself leading a creative collaboration, your chosen tone and register create the initial atmosphere while the stylish use of language can keep participants engaged and help them make sense of their ideas.

Conclusion

Language at the most basic level – choosing words and putting them into phrases and sentences – creates effects that enrich and focus meaning. But engaging through language also encompasses appealing to the imagination with detail and creativity. Claire S. E. Cooney and Carlos Hernandez use the term 'muscular velocity' to describe language, verbs in particular, that leap from the page. No matter what you are writing, words can be 'unexpected, surprising, powerful in a way that grabs the reader' (Cooney and Hernandez 2022). This tells us that while words position a relationship with the reader, they can also create particular aesthetic effects: sparking the imagination, directing and sustaining interest and making meaning.

Style also serves to embellish and reinforce the other domains we have considered so far, giving insight into how the setting, plot and characters function, highlighting themes, manipulating the pace and conveying key concepts. Often in our short stories and novels, we think about the ecology of language: how the metaphors and figurative language we deploy work together to convey the sense they are part of the same system. For example, when Helen was working on a draft of her novel featuring an Australian astronaut voyaging to Mars, she decided to deliberately draw on imagery that evoked the landscape of her character's homeland, eschewing comparisons to North American flora and fauna. While the technique may not be obviously apparent to many readers, subconsciously it still produces aesthetic effects which frame the character and her particular way of seeing the world.

Many style guides pitch academic writing – and consequently academic discourse more generally – as neutral and objective, to such an extent that Helen Sword argues the title of her book *Stylish Academic Writing* seems to be an oxymoron. Why, many academics might ask, 'should we accessorize our research with gratuitous stylistic flourishes? Doesn't overt attention to style signal intellectual shallowness, a privileging of form over content? And won't colleagues reject as unserious any academic writing that deliberately seeks to engage and entertain, rather than merely to inform, its readers?' (2012: vii). Yet, ultimately she argues, and we agree, that 'elegant ideas deserve elegant expression' (ibid.).

Often, simply paying attention to words is enough to begin using them more powerfully. You can keep a word journal, for instance, where you write down words or phrases you encounter that provoke your curiosity or create impact. This will not only improve your control over your written expression but will also enrich your success with public speaking. The right word to switch register and arrest attention, the right word coined for the right idea, the right synthesis of ideas elegantly expressed can make a huge difference for audience buy-in. Luckily for you, the way to upskill yourself with effective word choice and organization is by reading lots and lots of beautiful poetry. We recommend Tennyson, Keats, Rilke, Rimbaud, Plath, Neruda and Angelou as some excellent starting points. While it may not be possible to choose your words as carefully when facilitating research collaborations as you might when sitting down to write the results, an awareness of the power of language can still help you communicate more effectively with your audience, evoke and acknowledge the complexity of the ideas at play and give a shape to the overall experience.

THE DEFENCE INNOVATION BRIDGE: A CASE STUDY IN SEARCHING FOR A COMMON TONGUE

The project

The Defence Innovation Bridge was a funded collaboration between the University of Queensland's Business School and the Department of Defence to trial a new model for innovation, giving Defence personnel space to identify problems that could be solved with innovative applications of off-the-shelf technologies. The resulting full-day Story Lab brought together researchers in disciplines ranging from robotics and cybersecurity working together with Defence personnel and industry experts from start-ups and large corporations like Boeing.

The challenge

In designing our Story Lab, we aimed to leverage the power of transdisciplinary teams as an important aspect of foresight and strategic planning in Defence. To do this, we had to work out ways to strengthen group cohesion and develop shared metaphors within the workshop and a shared language not only capacious enough to allow participants to communicate their expertise but also accessible enough that it would not dampen participation or create unintentional disciplinary hierarchies (Gilligan 2019). This balance was particularly difficult to achieve because Defence personnel regularly use jargon and acronyms unfamiliar to researchers and indeed researchers often rely on disciplinary frameworks and language which may not be shared outside their fields and may also have embedded assumptions. To counter, these are the questions we asked ourselves:

- How could we prime participants from different backgrounds to participate in a creative conversation?
- How could we minimize possibilities for pre-existing hierarchies to dampen participation and creative risk-taking (e.g. between graduate students and professors, or between military personnel of various ranks)?
- How could we create a shared sense of the problem that invited participants to continue to collaborate?
- How could we develop a shared language that was accessible to all participants?

The approach

We decided to use a shared storytelling activity – a near-future scenario in which the participants took on the role of different characters responding to a crisis – as the centrepiece of the workshop because stories are themselves rich, information-dense vehicles for communicating experiences. But in setting up this activity, we used a variety of techniques to set the tone for our Story Lab including:

- writing introductory emails in plain language to set the tone of the workshop as something different from a conventional workshop or academic conference;
- ensuring any briefing materials or workshop handouts avoided acronyms or highly specialized language;
- dividing the workshop into small groups, aiming for gender balance (where possible) and a good disciplinary or organizational mix;
- switching between instructional language to initiate activities and narration during the central scenario in order to immerse participants in the storyworld and re-connect them each round with the thrust of the action;
- being mindful of jargon within the workshop and regularly either 'translating' comments or requesting speakers to clarify and reframe their thoughts;
- introducing and encouraging humour;
- concluding with an innovation-themed exercise called 'Q's Workshop', a metaphor borrowed from the widely known James Bond movies, to help participants frame their suggestions for potential solutions.

We were pleased to note that participants, when guided, were able to effectively 'code switch' between styles of language. A select group of students from the Masters of Business Administration programme, focusing on 'Entrepreneurship', attended the workshops and ultimately teamed up with some of the experts and dedicated their efforts throughout the following semester to developing business cases for potential technological solutions arising from the challenge prompts identified during the Lab.

5

Risk, safety and a magic circle of awesomeness

Introduction

In July 2019, Helen took a major risk by moving from England to Australia for a new job in creative writing at the University of Queensland, based on a recommendation from Lisa. Less than a year later, a global pandemic closed borders and isolated Helen and her husband from friends and family. Helen vividly recalls watching Kim empty her office in preparation for lockdown, jokingly saying, 'See you in six months.' It was surreal.

To find a way to anchor herself in the months that followed, Helen suggested playing a Dungeons & Dragons-style roleplaying game over Zoom. The game had minimalistic rules and a loosely scripted story, relying on 'pinball mechanics' where players made choices, rolled dice for success and faced consequences. Every two weeks, the players met up online to tell stories about a fiercely belligerent dwarf, a befuddled book-worm mage who never got her spells right and a half-mermaid enchantress with a voracious appetite. In a time of unrelenting greyness, drudgery and doom-scrolling, the game was awesome.

When we say the game was *awesome* we draw on the work of the philosopher Nick Riggle. Awesomeness, he argues, comes during moments in which we break out of our norm-governed roles to express ourselves – when we play, explore, take risks and imagine – creating what he calls a 'social opening' that invites others to join us and build a community, 'however small, of mutually appreciative individuals' (2017: 24). Being awesome is about doing something unexpected that not only shows who *we* are but also invites others to join in and show who *they* are, too. 'Our love of awesomeness,' Riggle argues, 'is an expression of our hope for a better social culture – one that is more imaginative, creative, and communal, and one that promises to bolster, enhance, and even help to realize the kind of free, just, equal, and diverse society we aspire to' (ibid.: 15).

Part of what made those storytelling sessions so awesome was that our group took risks together. Kim and Lisa were roleplaying for the first time. As three women from highly competitive fields, we were all exposing ourselves: as novices in a new form, as potentially 'bad' artists. Sometimes we chose deliberately foolish, character-driven actions if we suspected it might take the story somewhere interesting. But as we played, the sessions took on the same feeling of a giant game of 'yes, and'; the rhythm of offers, acceptances, and spurring imaginative leaps that drove the story forward, encouraged wild plans and even wilder outcomes, and forged deep friendships. Sometimes the sense of awesomeness arose from epic wins – an outcome so extraordinarily positive we had no idea it was even possible until we achieved it (McGonigal 2010). Just as often the awesomeness came from epic failures – when things went really, really wrong. The best sessions teetered on the edge of chaos. But in the game world, failure was never a narrative stopping point; rather, failure opened up new possibilities and revealed new threats. That is, our group 'failed forward', to use a term from gaming culture. We framed failure as interesting and exciting, an opportunity to test ourselves and explore our environment. Looking back, our shared interest in the project that led to this book was very much formed by those sessions as was the mutual sense of respect, trust and commitment that has seen the project develop.

We place awesomeness at the heart of this chapter because that feeling we had while playing together is *exactly* the kind of feeling that permeates the best Story Labs. It is the feeling that prompted one of our participants, as we approached the end of a session, to shout: 'No no no, we can finish this game, we can solve this, we can *win* this!' Her words encapsulate that sense that everyone in the room is doing work that interests, excites and at times confounds them, that encourages them to bring their experience to the table and to think about what they know (or think they know) in a different way. Riggle's grand theory of awesomeness is a good starting point, though we believe we can extend and nuance it further. Importantly, while it embraces aesthetics and art practice, it is ultimately more focused on social interaction. But we argue that various kinds of artistic practice and even artistic artefacts can also by extension create their own social openings, both by breaking out of the norms associated with them – genre norms, for example – and inviting participants and observers to likewise respond authentically and creatively. Certainly, each of the co-authors of this book has had the experience of reading a novel that challenged the way they thought about the world, with its repercussions bleeding out beyond the pages and inspiring them to approach their lives differently.

We expect by this point that you will already see some useful overlap with some of the concepts and approaches we discussed in Chapter 4, which encouraged you to think about how language can build a rapport with collaborators. In this chapter, we will examine some specific strategies for building an *awesome* group dynamic, one that encourages creative risks.

Creating a magic circle of awesomeness

The social norms that govern participants within their typical organizational environment are often very different to those of a Story Lab. As Finn and Wylie (2021: 7) argue, creative workshops are special experiences that function under their own set of rules and encourage attendees to be fully engaged, rather than distracted by their everyday activities. They also, in the best cases, erase the statuses of those in the room or at least diffuse those status-seeking and status-competing activities that close off social openings. Riggle (2017: x–xi) identifies various personas which might embody what he calls 'suckiness' (the opposite of awesomeness): the stick in the mud, the bore, the self-promoter, the douchebag, the fake ass person, the blowhard, the braggart, the thunder stealer (his list goes on). Without being taxonomic, we identify our own set of difficult behaviours that might require active facilitation strategies in Chapter 7, but the important point here is that many of these personas are characterized by *behaviours* that may be successful (in some form or another) in a day-to-day work environment. The stick in the mud, for example, might have developed a cautious attitude towards risk-taking after witnessing failure while the fake ass person might have adopted strategies to mask who they really are because they don't feel as if their authentic self will be welcome.

In order to encourage participants not to 'suck' (that is, to suck the energy out of the room), we have found it useful to think of the Lab as being bound within a magic circle. This is a concept commonly used in the field of game design (e.g. Huizinga 1995) whereby a social boundary is created by participants' willingness to suspend disbelief and accept the rules and conventions of that space as real. When participants in a workshop enter the magic circle, we look for ways to encourage them to temporarily set aside their real-world identities and concerns in order to engage with the activities on their own terms, without fear of consequences. This can create a deeply satisfying sense of immersion and engagement. We see the magic circle as offering a good model because it articulates the mindset participants need to adopt to enjoy a safe environment where they can step out of their comfort zone and take risks.

Creating a magic circle does not happen automatically. It relies on agreement, consent and mutual understanding. Below we offer some steps that are useful for anyone setting up a Story Thinking collaboration to consider as they create their own magic circle:

- **Establish the boundaries**: This could be as simple as identifying a physical space or setting specific rules for participation. It can be useful to choose spaces that are unusual (a new building, outdoors, etc.) or to arrange a familiar space in a new way. In some cases, props can help.

- **Communicate the rules**: Clear communication about the rules, objectives and expectations ensures everyone is on the same page. When participants unused to creative activities come to our Story Labs, we frame what we are doing so the value will be clear in a language they understand. This may mean code-switching between our natural language and the language of their discipline or organization.

- **Encourage participation**: Use active facilitation to engage all participants, so they feel invested in the work. This may require a range of strategies: seeing the whole room rather than focusing on the faces of a few participants, interpreting body language, making jokes, setting participants at ease and inviting them in, adopting deliberately inclusive tactics like allowing women to answer or ask a question first and maintaining balance with respect to gender and seniority of contributors (Carter et al. 2018). Appropriate choice of warm-up activities can also help.

- **Set the mood**: Create an atmosphere that supports the formation of the magic circle. This could include lighting, music, Zoom backgrounds or other sensory elements. As we discussed in Chapter 4, we have found it useful to allow the sensibility of our Story Labs (playful, creative, disruptive, enthusiastic) to permeate our email communications and briefing documents, our PowerPoints and even our clothing and communication style. We do love to dress up!

- **Enforce the boundaries**: Ensure all participants respect the rules and guidelines operating within the magic circle. This can be done by gently providing feedback when necessary, supporting and praising positive interactions and manoeuvring around negative ones. Don't alienate participants who may simply be working out how to behave or carrying over strategies from their ordinary lives.

- **Cultivate herd competency**: If you can't allow participants to self-select when joining the Story Lab, then try to ensure that you have a sufficient number of enthusiastic participants to create momentum and help establish and reinforce norms within the magic circle. We often designate group leaders in advance to help provide extra facilitation and discussion guidance if we anticipate an audience where we may face resistance.

By following these steps, it's possible to create a magic circle that allows participants to fully immerse themselves in a game or activity and experience a sense of separation from the outside world.

Creativity, risk taking and leaps of faith

When we discuss taking risks in this context, it may not be immediately clear what we mean. Some of the risks that people may take when thinking creatively include failure, rejection or criticism, uncertainty about how to work with incomplete or ambiguous data, and vulnerability. Two of the biggest risks participants feel are that the work may not be obviously useful and that they themselves might look silly. Both of these perspectives can create different kinds of resistance. As creative writers we recognize that one of the value propositions of our work is that 'the possible is our playground' (Wilkins, Bennett and Marshall 2023: 3) yet we have noticed some participants are particularly resistant to ideas or suggestions that are seemingly implausible. They may feel more comfortable with what we have elsewhere called a realist-rationalist approach, which can 'set a speed-limiting device on narrative impulses' (Marshall, Jennings and Anderton 2023: 13). This is often the tone of hard science fiction where narratives are bedded down with facts, details and explicit extrapolations. Fantasy writers, on the other hand, tend to be more comfortable working with associative logic and metaphor, so long as it is interesting and generative. A Story Lab may oscillate between different tones and approaches, but it is worth bearing in mind a participant invested in a realist-rationalist approach may find wild imaginings disrupt their immersion in the Story Lab. Put plainly: if the ideas suggested are too outlandish, some participants may disengage from the process.

This doesn't necessarily mean that you should veer away from the implausible or the imaginative, just that you should be aware of possible resistances and think about how to bring those participants along with you. Different strategies might include referencing authorities those participants respect, citing research on creativity, clearly signposting any shifts in calibration between activities, and articulating how activities link together and what results they are expected to produce. While it is easy to pay attention to and deliberately try to win over those who seem resistant to imaginative work, there are dangers in calibrating too narrowly to the plausible. Those participants at the other end of the spectrum may find a realist-rationalist approach straitjacketing and may start pushing back by introducing increasingly implausible or 'out there' ideas to entertain themselves.

Beyond this, we feel it is important to emphasize the particular value of creative thinking that pushes people outside of their comfort zone. A substantial body of research suggests creative thinking improves problem-solving, increases innovation and competitiveness, enhances cognitive flexibility and resistance to 'future shock', improves mental health and produces better learning outcomes as individuals make new connections between seemingly disparate ideas (Fletcher and Benveniste 2022). Exploratory work is valuable precisely because it produces insights that are often hard to come by with more direct, incremental or more overtly solutions-driven approaches. This echoes François Jacob, who shared the 1965 Nobel Prize for Physiology and Medicine with André Lwoff and Jacques Monod, that science need not only be driven by rigorous hypothesis testing or practical solutions. There is a kind of science – which he calls 'night science' – that 'wanders blind. It hesitates, stumbles, recoils, sweats, wakes with a start. Doubting everything, it is forever trying to find itself, question itself, pull itself back together. Night science is a sort of workshop of the possible where what will become the building material of science is worked out' (Jacob 1998: 126). Researchers Yanai and Lercher build on this, arguing that 'the creativity that we find in this realm is not only needed for the generation of novel hypotheses but also, for example, for the development of new methodologies' (2019: 2). It may be easy to reduce this sense of 'night science' to the broadly imaginative or the inspirational in its classical sense, an idea breathed into you by some outside force or indeed your own subconscious. But our own artistic practice has taught us to question this model of inspiration. We find that this bold, questioning, doubtful, imaginative mindset comes from a willingness to take a leap of faith that the insights and less tangible benefits gained from this work are worth the time.

Psychological safety mechanisms

There are particular kinds of emotional risks that may go beyond those we have already discussed. Here too we draw upon work done within game design where practitioners have articulated various safety mechanisms that can help participants process uncomfortable or difficult feelings raised by creative work. For example, Helen designed a narrative game to embed in a Story Lab aimed at helping transdisciplinary researchers imagine the social and environment pressures that might lead to a collaborative project's success or failure. When 'play-testing' the game with Lisa and Kim, one prompt asked Lisa to imagine an instance in which she might have a falling out with another member of the team. Lisa became visibly upset as she was forced to imagine a scenario where she might let the team down due to her overloaded commitments. The roleplay was valuable in that it helped us as a team explore an important threat to the project's success (overwork), but it also prompted us to deal with some genuinely powerful emotions. While such instances are relatively rare in our experience, that was not the only time creative imaginings have led to deep wells of real feeling, particularly when they touch upon the actual social dynamics, values and judgements of people in the room. Even roleplay with created characters can generate complex responses.

Beyond more obvious forms of distress, we are aware from our own experiences that workshops often raise issues related to participation consent and anxiety about being judged or fear of public speaking. These issues can create barriers to learning and participation and it is important for facilitators to be aware of them. Just as the magic circle is a useful concept we have adapted from game design, so we have repurposed various safety measures that may be used. These allow participants to momentarily detach from the activities – to step outside the magic circle – while still allowing those activities to continue. These include:

- **Advance briefings about sensitive topics (including interpersonal dynamics)**: If the facilitator expects in advance that a topic may give rise to sensitivities, it may be useful to establish ground rules for participation, discussion and stepping away in advance. This could also involve identifying or allowing for self-identification of vulnerable participants in advance so that everyone can approach the topic with suitable care.

- **The x-card**: The x-card is a physical card that can be held up by a participant to indicate that they are uncomfortable with the current situation and wish to stop or change it.

- **The okay card**: For situations where you think participants may want to discretely signal discomfort, you can lay out a card by an exit. If a participant taps the card while exiting, it signals they are fine. If they don't tap the card, it signals a facilitator should come out to have a private conversation. This is obviously most useful in smaller groups where the facilitator can keep track of all participants.

- **Warming up**: A slow, staged warm-up can help participants relax and become comfortable with doing creative activities while getting to know their groups.

- **Comfort (and discomfort) breaks**: Regular breaks may be scheduled to allow the facilitator to get feedback or to create space for further discussion privately if necessary.

- **Offering options for participation**: Providing a range of options for participation, such as written responses or small group discussions, can help participants who are anxious about speaking in front of the group feel more comfortable and engaged.

- **Providing additional structure in activities**: Free-form activities requiring spontaneous response may be discomfiting to some participants. If you expect participants might be uncomfortable, consider whether your activities may need additional 'guard rails' (instructions, limited choices, templates, etc.) that can guide people if they need it.

- **Emotional support and after care**: Depending on the context, it may be useful to provide emotional support resources for participants, such as designated safety officers, counsellors or trained professionals who can offer support or guidance.

Specific emotional safety measures may not be necessary for many styles and topics of Story Labs, but it is always important to consider what will make a safe and comfortable environment for participants. It is worth noting that while safety features can be useful, they can also create the impression that an activity is 'unsafe'. This can create the opposite to the intended effect, triggering or contributing to anticipatory anxiety (Jones, Bellet and McNally 2020). Likewise, some research indicates that content warnings often have no effect (Bridgland, Barnard and Takarangi 2022). As a result, we often choose approaches that are light on advance signalling but rely more heavily on active facilitation if problems arise. If you have not introduced explicit mechanisms such as content warnings or an x-card, then you should consider what activity or content might provoke negative reactions and what you will do in a situation where a participant is discomfited.

Ultimately, we feel it is useful to distinguish between being psychologically safe and being psychologically comfortable. It is important that all Story Labs are safe environments and it is our duty as facilitators to ensure to the best of our abilities that we take safety – psychological and otherwise – seriously. But while comfort may be useful at times, so also may discomfort. The work of INSEAD Assistant Professor of Organizational Behaviour, Li Huang, suggests the optimal recipe for fostering creative cultures could involve a foundation of psychological safety coupled with minor disturbances to the existing norms, such as those prompted by sarcasm (where a participant must work out the discrepancy between what is said and what is intended) and directed curiosity (when a participant focuses on a specific difficult task) (Huang, Gino and Galinsky 2015, and Hagtvedt et al. 2019). What links these elements is that they prompt an 'atypicality mindset' where we effectively trick our brains into perceiving a unique scenario that demands innovative responses and solutions – where we can't just coast on our regular patterns of thinking and behaving. From our own experience, because these activities can be so immersive, engaging and cognitively demanding – more than a standard academic conference of a similar length – we suggest scheduling shorter days and slightly longer breaks for recovery.

Conclusion

As creative writers we seldom think about our work as inherently risky: failure for us tends to mean at worst lost time and bruised egos. And yet the experience of both designing and playing our own Story Lab activities challenges us to look more closely at our own research journeys as fraught with the potential for failures. Research projects fizzle or run out of steam; granting agencies reject funding bids; critics pan novels that have taken a decade to write; junior colleagues fail to land permanent jobs or longed-for promotions; senior colleagues take on more responsibility, with ever higher stakes. This, we surmise, is why simply playing a game that simulates setbacks can cause intense emotions. As Kate Douglas argues in '"Not Another ARC Summer": Grant Applications and Life Narratives of Motherhood', her moving account of the challenges of juggling personal and private identities: 'It is very risky to present a vulnerable self in academia at a time when job insecurity is high and expectations around work hours are excessive' (2024: 109–10). For many researchers, our careers are bound inextricably with our sense of self. In a competitive and sometimes cut-throat institutional environment it can be difficult to acknowledge vulnerability or lift our heads from the trenches to imagine a different pathway, a different way of being.

And yet research from crisis situations ranging from Hurricane Katrina (Metzl 2009) to Covid-19 (Hildebrant 2021) emphasizes the importance of creativity for resilience. Nigel Hartley in his work on creativity and palliative care reminds us that in times of crisis, '"doing the next thing" will simply be forging the next step, taking the next breath, or speaking the next word … Simple acts are larger, louder, broader and deeper than before and a more intense feeling of self-consciousness emerges. This forces the self into the open, exposed and witnessed as both raw and vulnerable' (2007: 282). Reading this, we found resonances with times of emotional paralysis in our own careers where we felt under immense pressure to keep moving forward with our work, through moments of stark, confronting failure, ill health or emotional turmoil. In periods of challenge it has felt incredibly risky to move sideways, or backwards, or even to allow ourselves to stop moving at all – to pause, survey our surroundings and assess the situation.

Yet, as Hartley himself argues, art is inherently about a process in which one action creates the space for the next. When we write, one word leads us to the next; sentences build into paragraphs, into stories. Sometimes we find the right words the first time but often we don't – we return, revise, have another go at it, a little bit wiser, a little more certain. To draw on the words of the poet Gloria Anzaldúa:

> Writing is like pulling miles of entrails through your mouth. Why the resistance?
>
> Because you're scared that you won't do it justice. Because it'll take time, and there's no guarantee that you'll be able to pull it off. Because it is stressful and exhausting. … Writing also involves envisioning and conceptualizing the work and dreaming the story into a virtual reality. The different stages in embodying the story are not clearly demarcated, sequential, or linear; they overlap, shift back and forth, take place simultaneously.
>
> (2015: 102)

For us, as researchers and practitioners ourselves, writing has modelled a broader process of embracing and navigating risk in our work, asking from each of us our own leap of faith. This is difficult work – but we also know that it can lead to extraordinary insights and outcomes as well. For just as one word calls forth the next, so one act of boldness and courage can encourage another, creating social openings that invite those around us to create moments of genuine awesomeness.

MOONSHOT: A CASE STUDY IN CALIBRATING CREATIVITY, RISK AND SAFETY

The project

Moonshot is a storytelling game we produced for the University of Queensland's Research and Innovation office. The game supports researchers embarking on collaborative major initiatives by exploring how that project might develop over a five-year timeframe while mapping out risks and critical junctures. One of the key risks to a collaborative project is the internal dynamics of the team, yet this risk has received relatively little attention. Long-term relationships between collaborators and the dynamics of these teams remain the 'black-box of collaboration study' (Jeong and Choi 2015: 460). Provisional research suggests three critical conditions for success: having a facilitative leader, managing professional differences, and being open to learning and cooperating with others (Edelenbos, Bressers and Vandenbussche 2017). In the best cases, long-term partnerships that manage both formal and informal communication can create positive feedback loops, with previous accomplishments leading to ongoing feedback and consistency in themes and organization (Ulnicane 2015).

The challenge

We wanted to use storytelling to model the internal dynamics of the team as members initiated projects, and the ways setbacks might lead to shifts in focus and organization. The game provides open-ended storytelling prompts that team members encounter as they imagine different stages of their project. For example, one prompt reads, 'It is difficult to secure the cooperation of important stakeholders. A project fails. Which one? Why?' The team member might announce that a community-led arts project failed because the partnering teachers at a local school didn't have clear ways to embed the project into their existing curriculum. Another team approaching the prompt with a different project might determine that their efforts to gain access to sensitive health data didn't pay off because the differing ethics requirements of the involved institutions didn't align.

In addition to these prompts, the game uses Tension tokens to denote situations where stakeholders or members of the project team didn't feel as if they had been appropriately consulted in the decision-making. This made visible the social dynamics of a research project. When a research project begins, unspoken concerns such as personal histories, personality clashes, status differences and uneven levels of investment are seldom addressed because participants aren't comfortable revealing them. In practice, we have observed participants are often most excited about using these Tension tokens because they immediately feel subversive and, as we discussed in Chapter 2, nothing creates stickiness of attention like a hint of conflict.

In preparing a preamble that would guide facilitators in how to introduce safety measures we asked ourselves:

- What safety measures might be introduced to manage adverse reactions? How could they be easily integrated into facilitation without creating unnecessary signalling about the risks of the game for an audience unused to creative activities?
- What impact might safety measures have on the intended value of the game? How could we calibrate between the usefulness of the game in exploring the internal dynamics and the safety of participants who might encounter confronting emotions?
- How could we identify what aspects of the game might feel unsafe to some participants? What strategies might be useful if we expected to encounter problems?

Our approach

We described several possible safety strategies that could be employed including discussing boundaries directly, discussing potential challenges in advance, x-cards and passing options, placing topics out of bounds during gameplay and using a variant of the game that allowed participants to place Tension tokens if they so chose but did not direct them to do so within any of the prompts.

In a standard session we imagined that the groups would be invited to list the potential challenges they were interested in discussing, which would guide group members toward topics that were deemed safe. All

players would be alerted to the fact they could pass their turn at any point
or retrospectively declare a topic or narrative advance out-of-bounds if
it made them uncomfortable. In situations where the facilitator knew a
group might struggle, perhaps because the internal dynamics were known
to be fraught with power struggles, a game variant which downplayed the
Tension mechanism could be used.

What we found was that a one-size-fits-all strategy did not always
work. As Stark (2014) argues in an essay about roleplaying safety, it can
be hard to know what is going to be hard and it can be hard to know
when a player isn't having fun anymore. In some games, teams with good
working dynamics might still find aspects of the gameplay emotionally
challenging, simply because they don't like envisioning failure or imagining
tension between team members or stakeholders. Some of these struggles
can be highly productive and, indeed, are part of the point of the game.
By better understanding their team dynamics, participants can come up
with strategies for addressing future potential conflicts in advance. In other
cases, the game had extraordinary emotional 'bleed', a term for the way the
emotions prompted by playing a character in a fictional situation might
spill over into the real world (Montola 2010).

One player saw her gamified self consistently derailed by managing
ethics and performing too many administrative roles, which stopped her
from doing the research that genuinely excited her. She hadn't thought the
Tension tokens would be an element her team members would draw upon
because they had been working together successfully for several years. It
was a surprise to her, then, how often she used them to represent tension
in the external environment. The game sparked the sense she was working
in 'hostile territory', as she described it. In the session itself she didn't
appear upset but afterward the realizations 'roll[ed] around in [her] brain',
prompting a difficult discussion with university senior management in the
days following. Reflecting afterward, she said the game was useful precisely
'because if it can encapsulate [a sense of the research environment] and
lead to a breakthrough … I will then have a better understanding of the
environment and a better understanding in an explicit and consciously
held view that can then be used to make decisions going forward'. But when
asked about safeguards, she felt it would have been difficult to introduce any
that would have had an impact: 'It's a little bit like saying how do we make
the game protect you from the reality that we're trying to approximate?'

6

Affinity, inclusion and forging fellowships

Introduction

In the last few years, a meme has circulated around social media. Although there have been variations, the most common was a photograph of Ian McKellen dressed as Gandalf, and the caption reads 'Use the Force, Harry'. It is difficult to unpack humour without killing it dead, but this meme helps us explain something not only about affinity and genre, but also about how widely spread genre affinity is in contemporary media. The joke works because it conflates three wise mentor characters out of popular culture as though they are interchangeable: Obi-Wan Kenobi from the *Star Wars* franchise, Albus Dumbledore from the *Harry Potter* franchise and Gandalf from *The Lord of the Rings* franchise. The humour comes in recognizing their similarities, but also their differences. The storyworld logics of Hogwarts, Middle Earth, and a galaxy far far away and long long ago are quite different, in a way that creates incongruity. One doesn't bring a magic ring to a lightsaber duel, and Sauron isn't going to be defeated by shouting *Expelliarmus!* In order to 'get' the joke, the audience has to be familiar with the characters and the worlds, recognize the similarities and differences, and potentially have an investment in at least one of those storyworlds (even as we wrote this introduction, we were prickling at the idea that a lofty character such as Gandalf would concern himself with boy wizards and Tatooine orphans). A meme is a very twenty-first century kind of joke: made to be shared with a presumed like-minded audience. It is no surprise how many times we saw this meme, given the number of geeky people we know. That is our community: the world of SFF nerdery.

However, you will note we used the word 'franchise' to talk about these storyworlds. There is nothing alternative or subcultural about any of these stories, even though they do spawn subcultures defined more by their intensity than their interest. While some fans may like to police knowledge (and humour) about their favourite SFF storyworlds, the once-specialized knowledge they value has moved 'from the invisible margins of popular culture and into the centre' of media consumption (Jenkins 2006: 12), or, as Michael Saler succinctly puts it: 'we are all geeks now' (2012: 3). So, the joke works not just in SFF communities, but through a general affinity with people who may be more or less attached to, or even openly impatient with, the storyworlds referred to. In essence, those storyworlds function as a common language or reference point, and the humour is available to most people at the moment they are invited in by being shown the meme.

In Chapter 4, we wrote about how aspects of writing craft – word choice, imagery, style and tone – have a role to play in engaging Story Thinkers' imagination and bringing them into common understanding, and in Chapter 5 we laid out principles for creating a safe environment to take creative risks. This chapter builds upon the work of both those chapters by exploring how some of the elements that underpin genre fandom provide a model for building and extending a common understanding to a common purpose. This commonality is particularly important when drawing together researchers from different disciplines and backgrounds. Schmidt et al. (2020) identify four arguments for inclusion: that those affected by research outcomes should have the opportunity to be involved in the process; that research co-produced between science and society leads to better outcomes; that it produces more legitimate outcomes; and, finally, that it enables collective learning. Kok et al. (2021) agree with the assessment that complex problem-solving teams work best when they include different stakeholders, values and perspectives, but, they argue, in practice balancing this diversity can create tensions. In the previous chapter we noted the difference between psychological safety and psychological comfort, and this extends to diverse groups. A 2009 study by Phillips, Liljenquist and Neale indicates that while homogenous groups may have a stronger sense of confidence in their performance and interactions, it is diverse groups that exhibit greater success in accomplishing their tasks, even though they are often less comfortable while doing so. Crucially, we want to signpost that this is not a chapter about 'doing inclusion' though inclusive strategies are important, as we discuss. Rather, we are interested in creating a dynamic that allows collaborators to identify as belonging to a group while also seeing what unique and valuable contributions they might make through their different perspectives and experiences.

Forging fellowships to battle adversity

James Paul Gee first argued for his concept of 'affinity spaces' in 2005. He proposed the term as an alternative to 'communities of practice' because he saw limitations (as we did in the introduction to this chapter) with the word 'community': for Gee, community implied membership and cohesion (2005: 1218). He was interested in finding nuance in the ways people related around shared interests when those people may be more or less invested, and approaching from multiple, even diverse, perspectives. In an affinity space, 'ongoing social interactions' determine what is possible, in a way that emphasizes process and shifting relations rather than rules and hierarchies. Gee's theory relates initially to education settings but has been adapted for online spaces (Curwood 2013), fan practices (Leppänen 2009), adaptation and remixing (Voigts-Virchow 2012), and digital literacies (Lankshear and Knobel 2007). These extensions and subtleties show in multiple ways how the social underpins the generation and transfer of knowledge, to the point where the social lays foundations for all else: 'researchers should attend to the socializing and other practices that may initially seem unrelated to the primary mission of an affinity space' (Lammers, Curwood and Magnifico 2012: 49). In other words, when Story Thinking in a team, attending to the social will maximize outcomes, because Story Thinking is a way of creating knowledge together.

Gee defines eleven features of affinity spaces that might be usefully divided into three concerns: concern with sharing and sociality (e.g. a sense of common endeavour, dissolving of hierarchies, porous leadership); concern with knowledge (e.g. generating knowledge, sharing knowledge, valuing knowledge); and a concern with multiple ways to engage (e.g. routes to participation, routes to status) (2005: 225–8). In other words, a good affinity space will be largely rank-free although it might have leaders from within, it will be generative and allow ideas to flow and be built upon in an egalitarian way, and it will recognize and value a variety of perspectives. In collaborative Story Thinking, attending to the logic of affinity spaces in these three ways enriches creative outcomes.

The uptake of affinity space theory in places where subcultures, especially fan cultures, thrive, suggests its particular applicability to science fiction and fantasy fandoms. SFF stories have a rare ability to create shared experiences that bring people together. For example, they can create their own languages to name unfamiliar things or to create a sense of defamiliarization or archaism that readers may find pleasurable (Mandala 2010: 1). These languages perform a function beyond the texts in that they are often used as shared knowledge to create affinity spaces that define in- and out-groups. For readers not versed in these genres, 'the estranging language … locks them out' but for those on the inside, language can function as a 'portal' to shared experience, like a code only known by an in-group (Wilkins, Driscoll and Fletcher 2022: 109). Many aspects of SFF stories and storyworlds have entered common parlance. May the Force be with you. Beam me up, Scotty. You shall not pass! Expecto Patronum. The Upside Down in Stranger Things; the ice wall in *A Song of Ice and Fire*, the back of the wardrobe in *The Chronicles of Narnia*. All of these references to SFF stories may not necessarily be loved by Story Thinking collaborative groups, but they are very often known.

Fan engagement with existing SFF texts is a distinctive aspect of the way SFF is consumed, talked about and circulated globally. Writing of George R. R. Martin's fans, Victoria-Uribe and González-Alcaraz show how 'the passionate fandom of the book series has taken to analyze every single detail of the books, seeking clues that could predict how the story will end' (2021: 14). This speculation is shared between fans without the synthesizing eye of moderators; its purpose is creating knowledge together; and it draws in multiple perspectives. Many fan affinity spaces are built around the storyworlds of SFF. Bailey speaks of the mythology of Tolkien's Middle Earth, for example, 'exert[ing] its own gravity, drawing in smaller stories (like *The Hobbit*) into its orbit' and while Middle Earth may be the 'dominant construction' (Bailey 1992) because it has the mark of the author upon it, many other people have used and repurposed that storyworld for their own ends, whether personal (fan art, fan fiction, cosplay) or commercial (tele-visual adaptations, Lego, peer-to-peer commerce such as t-shirts and book nooks on Etsy and eBay). The dissolving of hierarchies that the fandom is keen to promote (Wilkins, Driscoll and Fletcher do problematize this ideal) means that the creative work encompasses not just books published by big multinational publishers, but also by independent presses, self- and hybrid-publishing models, peer-to-peer fiction sites such as Wattpad and, of course, fan fiction. In the sections that follow we look at how the logic of those affinity spaces – rankless, generative, inclusive – can support better collaborations.

Rankless

Western ideas of leadership in groups are often codified socially rather than decided in the moment based on the activity at hand. Leaders often have names or titles that indicate their leadership (Sergeant, Professor, Your Honour). When entering a collaborative space for imagining, it can be difficult if not impossible to leave those hierarchies outside. We have noted this in our practice, especially working with entities such as the Australian Defence Force, where understanding and following the chain of command is deeply ingrained.

While dissolving rank altogether may be impossible, affinity space theory can help us think through alternatives to existing hierarchies. Because an affinity space is more porous than a community (where one might have to insist on a particular kind of membership or rules and thus alienate newcomers), there is room for inviting Story Thinkers in with an offer of common endeavour. It is therefore important that collaborations take the time to establish not only goals, but also the 'why' behind the goal.

Establishing a sense of common endeavour may be as simple as having participants talk about their own investment in the problem to be solved. Just as fan groups run on passion, so too can Story Thinking collaborations. As we laid out in Chapter 3, a character's 'why' makes a story compelling; so too can participants sharing their 'why' compel each other to invest *together*. When people bring affect to problem solving, external hierarchies cannot help but wobble: the most important people in a group may now be those who have the most enthusiasm, drive and creativity. Emergent leadership roles can be filled spontaneously, rather than based on ordinary markers of social rank. A deferential doctoral student can, out of an abundance of passion, become a blazing firebrand leader; an introverted assistant can, out of an abundance of creativity, take charge of a futuristic story's unexpected plot twists. As Lammers writes, 'It is important for affinity space researchers to acknowledge the differences in available leadership roles and to acknowledge that members sometimes invent new roles when the need arises' (Lammers et al. 2012: 49).

Another way to destabilize hierarchies is through humour. Humour is widely understood to help in 'boosting group morale, maintaining group consensus, and encouraging closer bonds between group members' (Tsukawaki et al. 2020: 416). Researchers call this 'affinity humor', which reminds us that while facilitators who crack a lot of dad jokes *may* have an impact on the mood in a collaborative space, the best kind of humour is that which arises out of the group dynamics and the activities and resources at hand. In our Story Thinking practice, we have worked with people who created and acted out flamboyant characters to the delight of everyone in the room, groups who killed themselves laughing over the ridiculous ideas they floated to solve problems, and witty callbacks that referred to exigencies such as technology failures on the day. Affinity humour is emergent and rankless, and enhances both a sense of inclusion and a sense of creative playfulness.

Generative

Story Thinking is, at its heart, a creative practice. We use the tools of creative writing to generate knowledge. We are often asking people who do not regularly participate in creative activities to come up with characters and build worlds and develop plots: and many are intimidated by this prospect. 'I'm not creative,' is something we hear often. Persistent ideas of what creative people are underpin this insecurity. Certainly, the Romantic notion of the individualistic, inspired creative genius pervades Western thought. If affinity is about sharing actions and ideas on cue, then how does that square up against that ideal of the creative genius conjuring up masterpieces alone in their garret?

Well, let's throw out the ideal. It's rubbish and it's also probably sexist, classist and racist. The reason Coleridge could wander on the moors and have dreams about Kubla Khan was partially because of wealthy patrons (the Wedgewood family), and a long-suffering wife who was watching their child (Sara), and an absence of structural impediments to his participation in indulgent creative drug-fuelled nonsense (he was a white guy). No matter what creative people tell you – and their myths mean a lot to them and can in some ways be enabling (Wilkins 2024: 9) – creativity is entirely materially and socially embedded.

Psychologist Vlad Glăveanu studied Easter Egg decorators in Romania to develop the concept of distributed creativity, that is a view of creativity that foregrounds relationships between people and people, and people and things: 'a view of distributed creativity precisely helps us overcome the old dichotomy of the "inside" and the "outside" and place creative action in the relational space created by the person's encounter with its social (and material …) environment' (2014: 38). While the paradigmatic model of creativity has placed 'strong emphasis … on cognition and individual attributes' (Glăveanu and Tanggaard 2014: 12), in fact creativity is thoroughly sociomaterial and thrives socially, especially in affinity spaces. Wilkins, Driscoll and Fletcher have written about this extensively in their work on 'genre worlds', showing that the social interactions (friendships, competition, collaboration, cooperation) of people invested in the same genre are a significant part of how the creative work gets done (2022: 95–131).

Affinity is created by generating knowledge together, and the social enhances the generation of knowledge. Ideas about singular creative identities – those individual geniuses who not only refuse to engage collaboratively but deride any intrusion of the social – run counter to this goal and need to be excluded from the Story Thinking enterprise. It is normal for people to feel intimidated by the idea of creating something from a standing start, but knowing they are doing it together with other people who are invested in their goals and who are not judging them can allow them to relax and play. Co-designing worlds, collaborating on plots and creating characters are all excellent opportunities for group members to contribute to a shared endeavour. We often find that groups who create characters become increasingly attached to them, eager to develop their histories or tell others about them. Likewise, if collaborators have created stories, they're often very eager to share them. Every time we have cut activities devoted to group sharing for reasons of time, collaborators have always pushed back.

Generating ideas is not just about the novel, but also about building on what already exists or what has already been suggested. The logic of the famous improvisation phrase 'yes, and' is important to articulate and teach in Story Thinking. Group improvisation is thoroughly social creativity: 'non-summative', 'irreducible … to the individual', and 'worked out … across the span of its enactment' (Hagberg 2013: 485). The phrase 'yes, and' reminds us of the two key components of creatively building on ideas. When we say 'yes' we affirm the existing idea. To say 'no' is to shut down possibilities, especially if the 'no' is delivered by somebody who, outside the Story Thinking experience, is more powerful in a hierarchy. When we say 'and' we commit to build on the idea, and as ideas get built, more possibilities are generated. For example:

> What if we genetically modified a worm to eat plastic?
>
> Yes, and what if we could also make it shit a substance that could be used as jet fuel?
>
> Yes, and what if every aeroplane had a worm colony on board, eating passenger rubbish and shitting fuel, so that we could constrain the environmental cost of transporting the rubbish and the fuel?

Certainly, they may be very silly possibilities, and the whole 'yes, and' endeavour can fall over like a Duplo tower, too tall for the two-year-old building it. But making the tower is just as important as reaching a perfect idea. It creates a sense of shared purpose, it makes participants more comfortable with risk, it shows participants how to 'play within the range of the idea' (Hagberg 2013: 485), it's fun and funny, and it allows glimpses of ideas that may turn into more concrete possibilities.

Inclusive

Haters gonna hate

Of course not everybody happily creates together, generating in-jokes and investing in a Story Thinking collaboration. The playful and informal nature of Story Thinking can leave some participants feeling neutral, suspicious or even hostile towards the kinds of creating and thinking they are asked to do. Sometimes, participants are expected to take part by their real-world hierarchies. While this can be difficult to negotiate in the moment, there is little that can be done.

Once again, fan culture gives us precedents for thinking through this kind of neutrality or oppositionality. In the introduction to this chapter, we wrote of how even the geekiest of memes is still accessible to people outside fandoms. As Gray notes, 'non-fandom is the comfortable majority … Being a fan requires discipline, whereas being a non-fan is considerably more open and nebulous a category and practice, involving considerable flow in and out of different viewing positions' (Gray 2003: 74). Participants who are neutral to Story Thinking, then, may play along readily enough but never show enthusiasm. It is important to remember this could be about the work they'd have to do to be enthusiastic, just as fans have to work to be fans. Moreover, neutrals might be good bellwethers of the flow of an experience, indicating where an activity or question relies too much on the passionately invested to carry the load. It may also be an indicator of where different perspectives may lie, and an astute facilitator of Story Thinking should always remain open to the value of different perspectives.

What, then, do we do about the haters? In fan cultures, considerable energy is expended in the practice of 'hate reading': that is, enjoying something through disparaging it. In fact, this can be another generator of affinity: haters often form social action groups or 'hatesites', and can thus be just as organized as their fan counterparts (Gray 2003: 71). Importantly, according to Gray, haters 'find cause for their dislike in *something*' (ibid.). That is, it is meaningful to them to hate something. By the same logic, if a participant is clearly or openly negative about Story Thinking, we have to assume two things. One, that there is a reason they hate it, and that reason may never be known to us. In our Story Labs we have had negativity made known to us, of course, but we rarely see coherent evidence that it is about us or about our methods particularly. But, secondly, and perhaps more usefully, studying the haters can provide 'insight into the nature of affective involvement, for many of us care as deeply (if not more so) about those texts that we dislike as we do about those that we like … Behind dislike, after all, there are always expectations' (ibid.: 73). The haters allow us to reflect on expectations, especially our expectations about affinity and affective engagement. Again, they make room for us to accept and honour diverse perspectives.

'Cool story, bro': why the hero's journey must die

When we consider the question of diverse perspectives alongside storytelling, especially SFF storytelling, we run into the assumptions that storytelling = Western narratives, or at least an assumption of the embeddedness of story in the Western episteme. No template of storytelling is more overidentified with essential story structure (again, especially SFF) than Joseph Campbell's hero's journey, also known as the monomyth (and that name alone should sound alarm bells).

Campbell has been criticized for 'oversimplification and ahistoricism' (Keller 1986: 54), 'freeze-dried reductionism, logocentric oneness … and ethnocentric valorizing of Western power' (Doty 2014: 146), and of course for its sexism: whatever Campbell says about the universal applicability of the monomyth – 'the whole sense of the ubiquitous myth of the hero's passage is that it shall serve as a general pattern for men and women' (Campbell 1949: 121) – as Nicholson notes, 'it is starkly obvious that at the journey's "zenith" or "central point" the hero is distinctly male' (2010: 187). We admit we are part of this hate-reading affinity group. Elsewhere, Wilkins has described the hero's journey as nothing more than a 'narrative taxonomy' (2019: 22), which offers little critical interest or traction.

The trouble arises when key texts in the SFF genre hit the marks in that taxonomy so readily. Frodo called to adventure by Gandalf, Luke Skywalker meeting his mentor, Celaena Sardothien facing her series of tests, and so on. But to present the monomyth as the optimal or even the only way to tell a SFF narrative (or to approach a Story Thinking experience) is to close off possibilities rather than open them. While we discussed the usefulness of story structures in thinking about plotting in Chapter 2, we recognize any assumptions about the naturalness or normalness of Western story structures (even conflict, which isn't a driving force in all forms of cultural storytelling) must be problematized. As Nii Ayikwei Parkes writes,

> nobody seems to question the normal, but writers and storytellers from the margins will have been affected by it without the word ever being mentioned. They will have been told that their stories aren't relatable, compelling, structured, of high enough quality, etc. And while these things may be true sometimes, often what gatekeepers, fully schooled in the 3–5–7s but not the prejudices underlying them, are saying is, 'I don't recognize your normal,' or, more authoritatively, 'I refuse to recognize your normal.'
>
> (2018: 36)

The 'normal' in this case – the Western, male, white monomyth – should have its position as the essentialized Ur-story questioned; allowing storytellers, and thus Story Thinkers, to look more broadly for the nuance and subtleties, methods and substructures, images and allegories of other forms of story.

We hold that this is especially true in SFF, agreeing with N. K. Jemisin's view of SFF writers as 'engineers of possibility' (2018). Living up to this lofty aspiration, rather than 'grudgingly' acknowledging the marginalized (Jemisin notes editors have told her to 'tone down my allegories and my anger') means opening our minds to other ways of imagining people, plots and places. Of course, structures that are instantly recognizable because they have been so often repeated make this work easier to write about and communicate, but a good Story Thinker is always on the look-out for breadth in which to flex practice. We acknowledge that we are three cis-het white ladies, all of us now middle class, writing this book and taking this Story Thinking concept to the world. We have so much to learn, and we already do this in practice by casting our net wider in what we read and view, and making room for diverse perspectives in Story Thinking, even (maybe especially) when they are uncomfortable for us.

Conclusion

While writing this book, we've simultaneously held two conflicting thoughts in our minds. As academics with many years of experience teaching university students, we're fully aware that group work is the worst. People of all ages – from diverse backgrounds; with different amounts of academic, employment, or even life experience; and exhibiting varying levels of enthusiasm – will be thrown together for a limited amount of time and asked to complete a specific task. Shrinking violets will want to shrink in these situations. Loudmouths will want to bray. Box-tickers will want to do the bare minimum. Eager beavers will start to build grade-saving dams. Flakes will flake. It's a difficult position to put these people in and it can certainly be difficult to manage. Why even bother?

Because as researchers and creative writers who have co-authored dozens of scholarly articles and works of fiction, we also know that collaboration can be the best. Writing together can be more efficient than going it alone. It often generates new or unexpected ideas, since we're constantly seeing things from someone else's perspective, getting fresh insights on potentially tired-out drafts. In many cases, two or three heads are better than one.

The best collaborations are grounded in a sense of shared purpose, shared goals, shared ideals. They're partnerships built on mutual respect. The three of us have had over a decade to oil the mechanisms of our collaborations so that they run smoothly, but time isn't the only thing that has benefited our work together: it's our friendship based on a long love of fantasy, science fiction, medieval literature, games, general nerdery and our own brand of weird humour. These elements of interest offer many touchstones for our scholarly and creative conversations. They frame how we pitch and develop our projects. They help us to understand our research – and each other.

But of course our approach to collaboration extends beyond our own practices to the wider work of real-world complex problem solving. Our aim in this chapter has been to convey how SFF fandoms model a concept of 'affinity spaces' with broad applications in this work. Affinity spaces are where individuals with shared interests, passions or goals come together to collaborate, share knowledge and learn from one another. They are characterized by the sense of a common bond among participants who let go of their rank to engage in collective knowledge building and, we argue, collective, distributed creativity.

FAMILIES, VILLAGES, TRIBES: A CASE STUDY IN BUILDING BETTER TEAMS THROUGH EXTRAORDINARY SHARED EXPERIENCES

The project

In 2023, we were invited to work with a large department at a comprehensive university on a very different kind of Story Lab to those we were used to running. While many of our Labs have been geared toward helping researchers explore possibilities for their own work or anticipating the challenges that might threaten it, this project aimed to build up the organizational culture of the professional staff that supported those researchers. To encourage communication between subteams after a restructure, this department had adopted the Family, Village, Tribe organizational model pioneered in the 1990s by Flight Centre (Johnson 2013) to foster a sense of personal and social identity that can be hard to find in large organizations. Our goal was to find a way to animate and concretize the model within an extraordinary shared experience. To do this we created a Live Action Role-Playing (LARP) game.

The challenge

Our initial research problem focused on how storytelling could aid organizational transformation, following Chlopczyk and Erlach who bring a narrative approach to such processes, arguing that 'organizational change can be understood as a change and a transformation of the stories told in and about the organization – about its purpose, development, history, and way of operating' (2019: 2). In previous case studies we have investigated how Story Thinking can aid in identifying future world states and the critical pathways needed to reach them. Our approach here was both similar and different: we were interested in enacting systems change, yes, but rather than using stories to imagine preferable futures instead we wanted to use stories to *reach* those preferable future states.

As we delved deeper into the project we realized Chlopczyk and Erlach's crucial insight was that organizations are bounded by stories, which socially construct their reality. We wanted to change not just the stories this group told about themselves and what they were doing, but the way they had set about making meaning. But in helping them recognize and change those stories, we found ourselves departing from Chlopczyk and Erlach, who suggest finding a balance between envisioning a new future while being grounded in daily operations (2019: 2). We felt as if the daily operations themselves had become the sticking point, as they left few of the staff with enough energy to do the broader creative work of imagining possibilities and narrating a vision for the work they wanted to do collaboratively. We asked ourselves:

- How could storytelling create a new shared identity for the group that would allow them to break free from their habituated social structures and roles?
- How could a shared adventure embolden them to take risks, embrace ambiguity and develop new patterns of collaborations?
- Crucially, how could we win over an overworked audience whose attendance was mandatory (a room full of potential haters) so they could enjoy the benefits of the experience?

On the last point, getting participant buy-in was the main stumbling block. We could design the best activity in the world but if people couldn't come to it with a sense of openness, we knew we may well have a disaster on our hands.

The approach

We gravitated toward Live Action Role-Playing because we felt it could help participants temporarily shift their identity as they immersed themselves within a character role. This would simultaneously model the kind of shedding of old roles, the 'unlearning' that Chlopczyk and Erlach argue is essential to organization transformation (2019: 2), while at the same time immersing them in situations which would resonate with but not replicate exactly those they were used to encountering.

We designed the experience around the Family, Village, Tribe model, dividing the group into literal families, who were part of villages, all bound together in a single tribe. We adopted the setting of a faux-medieval fantasy world (recognizing the problematics of the term 'tribe', particularly in an Australian context) and decided on a series of challenges the group would face, progressing from the local and escalating toward the communal. The initial challenge asked each family to negotiate to secure food and shelter to survive the coming winter (focusing on negotiation and resource management) while the final challenge offered a prophecy that the winter would only end if one of the families was 'no more' (focusing on ambiguity, problem-solving and distributed creativity – no one person could solve the challenge on their own).

Many of the participants entered the Story Lab under duress. We used techniques from the previous two chapters to craft our invitation (outing ourselves as geeks and showing vulnerability to reduce hierarchies), create a magic circle (using props and music) and ensure the participants felt psychologically safe (identifying group leads to provide gentle guidance, allowing multiple kinds of participation). The beauty of the experience was that after a scaffolded introduction of activities that included choosing family roles and creating a family banner, many participants let down their guard and really began to enjoy the experience. The first challenge offered an opportunity to use their creativity to negotiate with the Fates (or facilitators) for new resources (including one family who built themselves a swanky summer home and another who chose to specialize in growing 'magic mushrooms'). They came to recognize the value of both tangible resources (fish, cloth, etc.) but also intangible resources (knowledge, diplomacy).

Over the course of the game as challenges mounted they developed their own system to communicate across families, forming an impromptu council. This proved invaluable as they faced the final challenge. They fulfilled the prophecy by allowing one family to volunteer to give up their identity, its members joining the remaining families, each of which incorporated an aspect of their banner into their own – an extraordinary outcome that took collaboration, creativity and a willingness to sacrifice. (While we had anticipated this sort of resolution, we had also prepared for the very real possibility of failure, with scripted endings for a game that involved no decision being made, a rejection of the prophecy, or even all the families singling out one to be destroyed against their wishes.) After the workshop, our liaison with the department reported that the group had hung up the banners around their shared space, one of the first signs of a new shared identity she had observed.

7

The Dungeon Master's guide

Facilitators as Shapers of the Cosmos

Ten minutes to nine on a mild July morning in Brisbane.

Sunlight streams through the large bay windows of the Global Change Institute. We're fiddling with our nametags, which keep peeling away. Most of the other participants in the room have already abandoned theirs.

'Note to our future selves,' mutters Kim to Helen, 'let's shell out for lanyards next time.'

We both want to make the right impression and the nametags aren't helping. Milling around the workshop room are crew-cut military personnel, a handful of representatives from Boeing in business suits, and clusters of academics ranging from the sleekly coiffed to the more traditionally ruffled, with backgrounds in robotics, cybersecurity and international relations. A few MBA students mingle with our collaborators from the Business School. While pockets of conversation have formed around the coffee urn, mostly everyone looks uncomfortable.

We're a bit uncomfortable too, if we're honest. We've been juggling a global pandemic, research and teaching commitments while prepping for this Story Lab. Though we are experienced presenters, we're far more used to faculty meetings, writing classes or Humanities research conferences where we seldom hear the phrases 'grey zone conflict' or 'Landing Helicopter Dock' thrown around so casually. What will these participants make of us? What will they make of our activities?

A monolithic screen shuffles through PowerPoint slides. Our rules of thumb ('Notice more. Use everything. Let go') seem out of place above a corporate footer which reads DEFENCE INNOVATION BRIDGE. But those rules have become a touchstone for us, a way to bring our creative selves into all aspects of whatever we do.

It's time to get started.

First, there's an awkward thirty minutes of preamble with a 'big hat' over Zoom who's explaining the future of artificial intelligence in Defence. People start checking their phones, surreptitiously writing emails. Another note for our future selves: cut the intros. Get people moving, get them *doing*.

Then Kim steps up to the podium with a wide smile and a very direct gaze, delivering her spiel about the value of play. Next time we'll cut it from ten minutes to five, and then the time after from five to three. Short, sharp, and punchy enough to establish our authority then move on. As she launches into the warm-up, the mood lightens. Now the groups are racing each other to come up with improbable suggestions for how to use a fork in new ways. To comb your hair? As a sailing boat for ants?

Meanwhile, Helen thumbs through the character sheets and the rules we've printed for the matrix game – the centrepiece of the Story Lab. She feels a flutter of imposter syndrome when she sees the briefing sheets our Defence liaison prepared. Next time we'll scrap those as well – too alienating for a diverse audience. As we move onto the next activity Helen is up. She knows it isn't her job to be the smartest person in the room, to decode the acronyms Australians seem to love so much. Her job is to invite the people who have given their time and attention into a story: control its pace, manage its twists and turns, and find some sort of satisfying resolution that helps us all translate what we've done together into something useful.

In her mind blaze the words of the famous pioneer of game design, Gary Gygax (1979: 2):

> Certainly there are stout fighters, mighty magic-users, wily thieves, and courageous clerics who will make their mark ... You however, are above even the greatest of these ... the Shaper of the Cosmos. It is you who will give form and content to all the universe. You will breathe life into the stillness, giving meaning and purpose to all the actions which are to follow. ... Though your role is the greatest, it is also the most difficult. You must now prepare to become all things to all people.

The Shapers of the Cosmos – that *feels* right for the work she wants to do. Sow seeds of adventure, guide and inspire, present challenges and achieve extraordinary successes. And to do that she knows she will need to draw on her intelligence and quick thinking, wisdom and good judgement, humour and charisma.

And so that brings us to this chapter's work. In the previous sections of this book we have laid out the four domains of Story Thinking and offered strategies for attending to the group dynamics of a Story Lab. Here, we guide you through some practical considerations for running your own Story Lab. We give an overview of some specific activities you can use yourself, aligned with each of the four domains, as well as some guidance on how to integrate them for best results. We finish with three templates for Story Labs we have successfully run to show how we've assembled these activities into a cohesive, structured programme of activities.

Roll for initiative: how to get started

Running a Story Lab may seem daunting but we have found a 'Ready, fire, aim!' approach can help: that is, if you have an opportunity, then dive in and use it as a learning experience to direct your future efforts. As you become more comfortable with working with partners and running the activities we suggest or making up your own, you'll develop a better sense of what works. That being said, even the most adventurous, improvisational researcher-facilitators will benefit from some forward planning. Building on the approaches we have developed across the previous chapters, we recommend asking yourself some basic questions as you begin your preparations:

- What do you hope to get out of the Story Lab? What do you want to learn or clarify?

- Will the Story Lab involve the input of partners or collaborators? What expectations might they have?

- What will be the focus of the Story Lab? Is it a single technology or a constellation of technologies? A system? A research question or project? Will you need a specific geographic, temporal or organizational focus?

- What kinds of people can contribute the expertise you need? How can you include them? Will they participate remotely or attend face-to-face?

- How many participants do you need? How many can you reasonably facilitate?

- What kinds of backgrounds will they have? How comfortable or familiar will they be with Story Labs?

- How will you calibrate for plausibility in your workshop? Will some activities invite wilder ideas while others require a greater rein on imaginative thinking?

- Are you discussing any sensitive topics? What kind of safety mechanisms should you introduce?

- How much reading do you expect participants to do in advance of the workshop? What do they need to get started?

- What kinds of outputs will you produce (e.g. written scenarios, prototypes, action plans, or strategic recommendations)? How will you be sure these are legible to your partners and to your participants?

- How will you follow-up with collaborators when the Story Lab is over? Do you need a broader engagement plan to develop a sustained joint programme of research?

Jot down some initial thoughts to these questions and return to them as you read through the rest of this chapter. The sections that follow will help clarify your thinking and perhaps at times challenge it as well.

Basic constraints

Before embarking on a Story Lab, assess the basic constraints that may shape the experience, such as time limitations, available resources, and the physical space at your disposal so you can tailor the Story Lab and address any obstacles that may arise.

Length

- **One-hour Story Lab**: This length is perfect for introducing a specific topic concisely. It allows for a quick overview to spark interest and curiosity and an opportunity for participants to engage in a focused activity or discussion, often on a single topic. This format is particularly suitable for time-sensitive situations or when participants have limited availability. It is appropriate for face-to-face or online delivery.

- **Three-hour Story Lab**: This is a typical Story Lab length. It offers a more detailed exploration of a topic, with a balanced approach between information sharing and interactive activities. It is possible to scaffold a number of exercises and produce one or two useful outputs. This length is also appropriate for face-to-face or online delivery.

- **One-day Story Lab**: With ample time available, participants can engage in interactive sessions, group activities and individual exercises. This format allows for in-depth discussions, presentations from experts, exploration of multiple perspectives and the development of practical skills. There may also be time to produce more polished written outputs. This length works well for face-to-face delivery but will be challenging for online delivery.

- **Two-day Story Lab**: Here, you can sustain an extensive exploration of complex subjects or skills. Participants can engage in a wide range of activities, including hands-on exercises, case studies and group projects. This format facilitates in-depth discussions, skills-building exercises and the development of polished outputs. The longer duration also provides ample opportunities for participants to develop deeper connections, foster collaboration and build networks with fellow participants. This length works well for face-to-face delivery but will be challenging for online delivery.

Delivery mode

- **Face-to-face Story Labs**: Face-to-face delivery is typically the norm for creative workshops (e.g. Bell 2005; Schwarz 2008; Finn and Wylie 2021). This mode of delivery promotes better cohort building through in-person interactions, fostering collaboration and trust. With fewer distractions, participants find it easier to focus, allowing for deep engagement and sustained attention. You can also judge the mood, attention and enthusiasm of participants more easily. Additionally, the capacity for longer Story Labs provides more flexibility in which topics you cover.

- **Digital Story Labs**: Increasingly, organizations are interested in Story Labs that can be delivered digitally because they are low-cost and can draw in participants from different geographical regions (Marshall et al. 2023). This mode tends to be more cost-effective and participants benefit from reduced travel requirements. Furthermore, the virtual nature of digital Story Labs can help avoid 'group think' as participants are not physically present in the same room, enabling a wider range of perspectives through multiple modes of communication (presentation and chat sidebar, for instance) and preventing ideas from converging prematurely. However, digital Story Labs come with their own challenges. Flexibility with tools and platforms can be limited, requiring participants to adapt to specific software or communication channels and technological glitches or lags may disrupt the flow of ideas.

Choosing participants

The success of your Story Lab will inevitably depend on your participants as much as your structure and facilitation skills. As we discussed in Chapter 6, in most cases we recommend selecting participants from different disciplines and backgrounds, but we recognize that in some cases the participant pool will be fixed from the outset. The number and mix of participants you anticipate will often have a significant impact on the kinds of activities you choose.

Group size

Small groups – groups of twenty or less – are ideal. A single facilitator can easily guide a Story Lab of this size, gauge reactions to activities, clarify when necessary and adjust the pace. Medium groups – groups of twenty to forty – work well when you can divide them into small groups. We prefer four to six people per small group, often working on parallel problems or generating parallel stories, with opportunities for feedback. A single facilitator can manage a group of this size, but additional facilitators or assistants are useful. Often with larger groups we nominate group leads in advance to keep everyone focused. Larger groups may also require a division between content delivery (introducing exercises, for example) and hands-on activities.

Group experience

There is a significant difference in running a Story Lab for eager participants used to creative methods and reluctant or anxious participants trying these sorts of activities for the first time. The former will often require less explanation for activities and will be able to get into the creative work faster. The latter may need additional scaffolding of activities. Gentler introductions such as 'Arts and Crafts' can allay worries and allow people to settle in; alternately, playful activities such as 'Twenty Forks' can encourage them to enjoy themselves. Almost all groups are likely to have some participants who play board games, act in their local theatre or are amateur writers or artists. We try to identify those people early on and leverage their experience to provide leadership.

Group mix

With a relatively homogenous group of participants who know each other, you may not need an icebreaker or deliberate introductions, which can save you time. You may also be able to rely on these types of participants to communicate effectively with one another using specialized language. With a relatively diverse group of strangers from different disciplines, you will need to give time for participants – at least those working in small groups – to introduce themselves and what they do. You may also need to do some work around clarifying jargon and acronyms which may be impenetrable to you and to other participants.

Advice for facilitators

Know your role

As the facilitator it often isn't your job to contribute ideas beyond a few prompts to get the group started. Instead, provide positive feedback, affirm ideas to generate momentum and, only if necessary, gently restrain ideas which risk becoming too far-fetched. Model the energy you want the group to have. This is particularly important when delivered remotely as the energy level is inevitably lower (at least at the beginning).

Reframe your expertise

We often work with partners in fields where we lack specialized knowledge. Initially, we found this a stumbling block to our collaborations – how ought we to facilitate a group of experts when we're newcomers to their fields? As we've become more experienced, we have learned to reframe our expertise: fundamentally, we are experts in process, rather than product. Know your activities and what you want them to accomplish but recognize you won't be able to perfectly control what happens at each stage.

Rely on subject experts …

As intelligent and curious non-specialists, we rely on our collaborators to provide the context we need, often in the form of briefing sheets, summaries and articles. When facilitating, we push responsibility onto the group to debate issues of plausibility and possibility, and to fill in necessary context.

… but keep an eye out for jargon

Discussions amongst a diverse cohort work best with accessible language. Your own lack of specialized knowledge can actually be a good barometer for how clearly a participant has communicated. If you didn't understand a point, then it's likely someone else in the room didn't either. Sometimes you may find yourself doing the work of translating other people's comments into lay terms for the group. If you're struggling to do this effectively, it may simply mean you need to push this work back onto the participants themselves by asking them to repeat, rephrase or unpack what they have said.

Keep the energy up and the activities moving

During small group activities, monitor the flow of conversation and the progress on the tasks. For face-to-face Story Labs, wander discretely within earshot; for digital Story Labs, use online tools such as GoogleDocs, Miro or OneNote where you can see contributions. If groups fall behind, you may give them more time or choose to push on (which is why you need to know your activities well). You should be able to glance around the room (or at the videos in an online platform) and use the participants' expressions to monitor the group energy. In a face-to-face delivery, you'll likely see participants engaging right from the start but it may take longer in a digital delivery to see real enthusiasm. Don't take this personally. Working online has a higher cognitive load and you may see that reflected in the faces of participants, particularly when they're trying to understand instructions and use a new tool.

Manage adverse reactions

Adverse reactions range from hesitancy and discomfort to outright scepticism, dismissal or hostility, as we discussed in Chapter 5. Some behaviours may produce unintended adverse consequences even if they are well-intentioned.

- **The eager beaver**: An enthusiastic contributor can be extraordinarily valuable, particularly in the early activities, but can derail the discussion at later stages where you want wider input. Gently manage their enthusiasm and keep an eye out for hesitant participants who may also have valuable insights.

- **The grandstander**: Some participants really want to share their ideas or expertise and so can hold up activities. Try not to let anyone hog the spotlight and watch the time, particularly for activities where a group reports back. Cut people short if you need to.

- **The class clown**: The Story Lab is supposed to be fun and so jokes are encouraged! If someone gets carried away, though, it can lead to implausible outcomes. Love them for their enthusiasm but guide the group back.

- **The know-it-all**: You're likely to have serious experts in the field and you want their experience and knowledge. But some Story Labs need to push at the boundaries of possibility. In the early activities, try not to let someone's knowledge of the *current* state of the problem shut down conversations about where solutions might come from.

- **The genre enthusiast**: Many of the ideas that emerge in the Story Lab may have appeared in science fiction previously. Don't let one person's knowledge of a trope shut down the group's desire to discuss or make use of it.

- **The chief**: Sometimes an awareness of rank, status or hierarchy can dampen participation. If you suspect this might be the case in advance of the Story Lab, you could approach the participant and make them aware of your concerns, group all high-status participants together so the issue is contained, or find a way to reduce the perception of the status of the participant through humour. Use good judgement here.

Our assumption in managing these adverse reactions is that the participants are generally well-intentioned and, at most, simply unhappy about attending the Story Lab. There are two adverse behaviours which deserve particular mention.

- **The alternative thinker or conspiracy theorist**: If you are running a Story Lab with an open call to members of the community you may encounter participants who don't share the same fundamental sense of the world. Approach the situation with sensitivity and respect. Establish ground rules that promote respectful dialogue and focus on shared goals and encourage critical thinking, evidence-based reasoning and fact-checking, while managing time and staying on topic. The aim is to maintain a constructive and inclusive environment while maintaining focus on the Story Lab's objectives.

- **The hijacker**: If you are running a Story Lab with a large bureaucracy that feeds into policy-making decisions, you may encounter participants with specific agendas that prove disruptive. Again, establish ground rules up front and seek input from the group to bridge differences. In situations where a participant actively tries to co-opt a Story Lab, more extreme forms of facilitation may be necessary such as direct intervention, having private discussions to understand a participant's motivations and exploring ways to incorporate ideas without compromising the Story Lab's integrity. Reallocating roles and seeking majority consensus among participants can also help counter disruptive behaviour. In severe cases, you may need to consult the Story Lab hosts or the team who has engaged you for guidance and support.

The poor wizard's almanac: sample activities for your Story Lab

The activities we propose align with the four domains we have discussed in previous chapters. When we use exercises such as these, we often tailor them to the time available and the purpose they serve in the overarching structure of the Story Lab, so they tend not to have completely fixed forms. Here, we describe the basic elements of the exercise with ideas for how to use them. If you're seeking to tailor them or create your own variants, we recommend returning to the relevant domain chapters and reviewing the strategies we offer there for ideas on how to alter and troubleshoot them.

Engage exercises

Twenty forks

Divide the Story Lab into small groups and have each group quickly brainstorm twenty uses for a fork. This can be done competitively, if you wish, with a race to reach twenty. Next, have the groups cross out the probable uses and divide the rest into possible or implausible uses. Finally, have the groups choose one from the list of implausible uses and work out what would need to be done to make it plausible or workable.

We often use this activity to warm-up participants. The initial brainstorming session helps them to push beyond only the most plausible or ready-to-hand ideas and the time pressure stops them from thinking too hard about what they are doing and censoring themselves. The competitive nature of the activity can also produce a sense of internal group cohesion. When the groups begin to work with the possible or implausible uses, they learn how to calibrate their expectations. They also learn that some ideas that initially seem implausible can be recycled or amended.

Cabinet of metaphors

The activity asks participants to create a shared metaphor for the problem they are trying to solve. A metaphor can do the work of helping a group from different disciplines find a shareable way of talking about different facets of a problem, both within the group and to that group's external partners. For example, climate change is like a conveyer belt that seems to go faster and faster, with no way off and no way to slow down. The metaphor doesn't have to be perfect. In fact, having groups discuss where the metaphor breaks down can also be valuable. In this metaphor, what does the baggage on the conveyer belt represent? Is climate change really such a mechanical problem? The point is to encourage experts to share their insights in plain language rather than using disciplinary jargon and intellectual frames.

This activity could be used as a warm-up to help groups work out the dimensions of a problem. Ideally, the metaphor should be easy enough to understand that it can be effectively communicated – though some groups may well enjoy developing increasingly sophisticated or bizarre metaphors in order to underline the nuance of a problem.

Arts and crafts

There are many ways that arts and crafts can be incorporated into other activities. For example, when asking participants to develop characters, you might ask them to use magic markers to doodle designs on a pebble or to create a sketch on a cue card. We have laid out magazines for participants to cut up and rearrange to create timelines or posters. We've also encouraged groups to draw banners to represent themselves and their interests.

We often use arts and crafts when we seek to help participants settle into a Story Lab, to slow the pace and provide time for reflection, or to shift instruction styles for learners who may appreciate visual or kinaesthetic activities. As Huotilainen et al. (2018) argue, engaging with materials in the process of creation can assist in regulating our mental well-being by enabling us to enter a state of deep concentration and flow. It also provides a safe space for experiencing and managing failure and emotions, and for fostering social engagement. Likewise, as Ainsworth and Scheiter (2021) show, sketching can activate prior knowledge, increase attention and enhance subsequent recall as participants integrate new information into their long-term memory.

Inhabit exercises

Worldbuilding questionnaire

As a large group or in small groups, use several prompts to brainstorm the 'pillars' of a future or alternative world. These can include exploring economic, social, political and environmental developments. Poll the group to select one or two suggestions from each category to use as the basis for imagining a shared world.

This exercise helps groups co-create the basis for a future world, which can then be used as the setting for further scenarios. We have found it useful particularly for groups who aren't necessarily used to thinking about the future. It gives a limited number of focal points to play with which makes extrapolation easier. You can also use it to calibrate suggestions, discarding those the group deems unrealistic or frivolous. One warning is that sometimes particularly 'interesting' but implausible ideas can be selected through the polling simply because members of the group are curious, mischievous or excited by the possibilities. If your Story Lab is geared to produce only very obviously plausible possibilities, you may need to have the group explicitly exclude implausible ideas before you move to polling.

Encyclopaedia entry

This exercise encourages participants to engage in 'thick descriptions' (Fischer and Mehnert 2021) of a particular setting or context, describing geography, politics, local customs, legal systems and any other element that may be of interest to the Story Lab participants.

Whereas the previous exercise asked participants to use a few basic details to sketch out the broad contours of a world, this exercise asks participants to go deep while providing a fun and easy-to-grasp format for presenting written results. Facilitators could also use this format to generate a scenario setting in advance, as the building block for further character or plotting activities.

Map making

Use digital tools, a hired artist or very simple sketches in order to map out a particular world, setting or landscape which you intend to explore in other activities.

Maps force participants to understand space and geography in ways that are different from purely verbal descriptions. We often use maps if we are exploring scenarios where the setting itself may provide concrete restrictions and opportunities. For example, when playing a matrix game it can be very handy to sketch out or create in advance a map that helps all participants visualize the terrain. This prevents characters from taking actions that are unrealistic (say, moving from one location to another too quickly) and also reinforces a sense of spatial relationships (say, reminding participants that Canada and the United States share one of the longest borders in the world, whereas China and India share a disputed 3,380 kilometre border of difficult mountainous and glacial terrain).

Envision exercises

The storyteller's pre-mortem

In small groups, think ten or twenty years (or longer, potentially) into the future to imagine the end-point of a given set of events, often a worst-case scenario. Then work backwards to plot out a timeline of cause and effect using three or four prompts which can be fleshed out:

- Somebody made a BIG mistake

- Corruption went unnoticed

- The general public found their own, unexpected uses for the technology

- A system wasn't properly maintained

- The world changed, but the underlying assumptions of the technology didn't

- Money ran out

- Something completely out-of-the-blue, never-before-seen happened to the world

- Somebody with a lot of power downplayed a problem

- A tiny, seemingly insignificant thing was overlooked

- Everyone lost interest because something better came along

- A decision led to an unintended consequence

- An outspoken group came to prominence with a strong view that undermined the way the technology was viewed

- A plot point of your choice

This exercise combines two approaches. One is plotting. Often when people are asked to come up with a story or narrative, they make the mistake of simply listing events. What storytellers know is that plots exist in chains of cause and effect. That means that writers are always thinking about how one thing may lead to another, how this node here may branch out into many other nodes, how to sort through those and come up with the right balance of interesting and plausible possibilities. The second approach is a more traditional pre-mortem. Research shows 'prospective hindsight – imagining that an event has already occurred – increases the ability to correctly identify reasons for future outcomes by 30%' (Klein 2007). This exercise works best when analysed for areas of risk mitigation.

Future shock

In small groups, construct a timeline in five-year increments that follows a particular situation, problem or technology as it develops. You can offer prompts relating to slow, incremental changes as well as tipping points and black swan events to suggest what happens between each five-year point on the timeline. Sample prompts include:

- Many people become fascinated by another culture which they seek to emulate. What do they incorporate? How do they change it?

- The growth of a new technology begins to have an impact. What is the technology? What fields is it changing?

- The economy contracts significantly. What leads to the downturn? Where is the biggest impact felt?

- A situation slowly gets worse. How does a feature of the environment become more dangerous? What are people trying to do about it?

- A new group of people are gaining power. What do they want? How are they changing things?

- Many laws no longer appear to be serving society. What happens when they are struck down?

- A series of scandals forces people to think about the ethical principles that shape their society. What new standards are put in place as a result?

This exercise follows a more conventional approach to mapping out the future by progressing linearly through time. By moving in increments of five years, participants can make relatively realistic jumps in time, exploring how a changing world might have an impact on the scenarios they are trying to generate. Crucially, as the timeline progresses, the world will grow increasingly divergent from our own present moment while still allowing participants to understand the logic of how and why that world has changed.

Welcome to the multiverse

Sometimes we call this 'Let's Kill Hitler!' in reference to the common science fiction trope of a time traveller seeking to avert the Second World War by assassinating Adolf Hitler. Working with either of the previous two exercises (or, indeed, any other exercise that produces future scenarios), identify a critical juncture or turning point and use it to create a range of additional scenarios: one good, one bad, and one 'weird'.

This exercise can help participants learn to recognize turning points. It is easy for groups to fall into the trap of either dystopian thinking or indeed utopian thinking. Here participants can calibrate their ideas with more specificity and explore the range of possibilities, rather than getting attached to a single, evocative vision of the future. In particular, the 'weird' scenario frees participants up to explore unexpected directions, without making it the Story Lab focus.

Empathize exercises

Character questionnaires

In small groups, answer a series of questions about a character to develop a sense of their background, motivation, fears and capacity for conflict. There are many sample character questionnaires you can mine for inspiration, choosing a mixture of questions that might highlight characteristics that pertain to the problem-space you are exploring. Some sample questions include:

- What is your most cherished childhood memory and why?

- Describe your relationship with your parents. Is it positive or strained?

- What is your greatest fear and how does it affect your actions?

- Do you have any hidden talents or skills that few people know about?

- What was the defining moment in your life that shaped who you are today?

- How do you handle stress or difficult situations?

- What is your favourite book or piece of art, and why does it resonate with you?

- Describe your relationship with money. Are you a spender or a saver?

- What is your biggest regret in life and how does it haunt you?

- Have you ever experienced unrequited love or a broken heart?

- What is your opinion on forgiveness? Are you quick to forgive or do you hold grudges?

- Have you ever had a mentor or someone who greatly influenced your life? Who were they and how did they impact you?

- Are you a risk-taker or someone who prefers stability and security?

- How do you navigate conflicts or disagreements with others?

- What is your dream or ambition in life and what steps are you taking to achieve it?

- Do you believe in fate or free will? How does this belief shape your actions?

- What is your relationship with technology? Are you tech-savvy or more old-fashioned?

- Describe a significant friendship or relationship in your life. How has it influenced you?

- What is your favourite place in the world and why does it hold significance to you?

- Have you ever faced a moral dilemma? How did you handle it and what were the consequences?

Many of these questions map clearly onto topics such as physical characteristics, social milieu, fears and desires, and relationships, and so they allow you to capture basic features and motivations quickly. You can build out a more detailed sense of a character by also including idiosyncratic questions. For example:

- What do you remember most clearly about the garden of your childhood home?

- What advice did your grandfather always give you and do you follow it?

- You had a recurring dream when you were eleven: what was it?

- If you had the ability to time travel, which era or specific moment in history would you choose to visit?

Participants can incorporate these characters into narratives or other activities or use them as the base of written perspective-taking exercises or even roleplaying.

Journal entry

Working individually or in small groups, write a short first-person account of either a typical day within a future world (tied more explicitly to worldbuilding) or an extraordinary day when something important happens (tied more explicitly to plotting).

This activity can be used after the previous activity or an alternate character development activity to flesh out a scenario. It is particularly effective if the goal of the Story Lab is to produce a written output because the format (brief descriptions, limited dialogue, a natural structure) minimizes the need for much knowledge of writing craft.

Matrix game

A matrix game is a low-tech simulation tool used for scenario modelling and analysis where participants assume different roles or characters with objectives that put them in potential conflict. It is a cross between storytelling and scenario-building. Gameplay progresses in turns, each of which represents a period of time appropriate to the scenario. Within a turn, each player will have an opportunity to take an action of their choosing and make arguments for why they should succeed.

A matrix game often takes two or three hours to play through effectively and so it tends to form the centrepiece of a one-day Story Lab as we outline below. Matrix games are wonderful for generating discussions, exploring different strategies, and gaining insights into complex situations by simulating interactions and dynamics between various actors or entities involved in a scenario (Curry, Price and Mouat 2023). But, like many activities that involve some form of roleplaying, they also highlight decision-making and so can aid training in leadership, crisis management and ethical judgement.

A journey like no other: Story Labs structures to get you started

In the following section, we outline three sample Story Labs to demonstrate how activities can be timed and scaffolded effectively. These structures ought to give a sense of the arc of a Story Lab as it moves from introductions, warm-ups, discussion of basic concepts, to deeper imaginative work, finishing with sense-making and translation activities.

Families, villages, tribes: a half-day character-oriented Story Lab

Our collaboration centred around an immersive Live Action Role-Playing (LARP) experience, which we discussed in our case study for Chapter 6. Drawing inspiration from Flight Centre's organizational model (Johnson 2013), this Story Lab assigned participants to literal families, villages and tribes. Each family was given a distinct backstory and an area of expertise, such as weaving, hunting, shelter-making or tool-making. The participants were then given a series of escalating challenges that required them to learn how to work together in larger groups.

Here, we opted for a long introduction to allow participants to settle in as they worked their way through their family's legacy boxes: specially designed props that held a scroll with their family briefing sheets, sealed envelopes with family roles and natures, alongside pens and a fabric banner for them to draw on. Because of the limited time for the workshop, we incorporated the morning tea into the first challenge ('the last of the autumn fairs'), so participants would find it easier to mingle and move around the room, exploring the possibilities of what they could do. We assigned each of the challenges a progressively shorter period, recognizing the first needed to be the longest to give participants time to navigate the game mechanics and that subsequent challenges would benefit from time pressure. We used the debrief to pull out insights from the game and allow participants to transition out of their character roles and back into real life.

10:00–10:10   Introduction to Ahro

Welcome to the world of Ahro, where the towering mountain, dense forest, and winding river form a breathtaking landscape. But winter is coming, the worst winter in a thousand years. What will your family do to survive when the winds howl and the wolves are at your door?

We will introduce you to the world of Ahro and the rules that will govern our Live Action Role-Play (LARP).

10:10–10:30   Meet your family

Working in small groups, you will learn more about your family, their history and their special talents. While designing your own banner, you'll also have the opportunity to take on roles within the family. Who will be the chief, forging your family's strategy? Or the loremaster, ready to record your legendary exploits and relate them to the tribe?

10:30–11:30   Morning tea and first challenge

In Ahro, it is customary for families to gather together for the last of the autumn fairs. Some will haggle and trade and negotiate, while others – the hunters and the artisans – will hurry to secure what they can in preparation. While you graze, you and your family will work out how to find enough food, warmth and shelter for the long winter. At the end of the hour your family's lorekeeper will report on your progress.

11:30–12:00   Second challenge

'There is another tribe. They are hungry, like you. The Shatterspear Tribe is on the march. They will raid each of your villages and plunder your treasures.' Each village must work out how to deal with the raiders.

12:00–12:30   Third challenge

Disease will come. The crops will rot in the field. The Fates have spoken: 'Winter will end when one of the families is no more.' The tribe must decide how to interpret and satisfy the prophecy.

12:30–12:50   Final debrief

You will write down a single word or phrase to summarize your feelings about the experience. Working together, you'll also reflect on what you have learned about your strengths in collaboration and your ability to work together to solve difficult problems.

The Defence Innovation Bridge: a one-day innovation-oriented Story Lab

In 2020–2021, a partnership between the University of Queensland's Business School, the Department of Defence, and us led to the launch of the Defence Innovation Bridge, which we discussed as our case study for Chapter 4. The Defence Innovation Bridge aimed to connect Defence problem-holders with potential solution-providers such as researchers and industry experts. We explored a plausible near-future scenario using a matrix game, which we used to identify tactical challenges as prompts for innovation.

We developed the basic premise for the scenario and used other tools such as maps and character 'role' sheets as starting points for participants in consultation with our Defence liaison, recognizing that we wanted to spend less time on co-designing the parameters of the scenario with participants and more time on playing through. To warm-up, we gave 'Twenty Forks' an innovation-themed twist to get participants used to a problem-solution mindset desired by our partners in the Business School. The day ended with 'Q's Workshop' which asked participants to come up with their own ideas for new inventions or applications of technologies.

9:00–9:30   Welcome, introductions, set expectations

You will be introduced to creative exercises designed to help you generate rich and accessible narratives based on your expertise. These will inspire innovative solutions to real-world challenges you identify throughout the Story Lab.

9:30–10:15   Imagination warm-up: 'Twenty Forks'

This is a technique adapted from improv. How many problems can a fork solve? It will get you in a creative mindset, help you be comfortable with suggesting ideas and building on others' ideas, and also encourage you to think about the balance between possibility and probability.

Segue into follow-up exercise 'Super Forks'. Everybody goes through their list and ranks their suggestions as 'probable' problems that could be solved by a fork, and 'possible' problems. Choosing one of the 'possibilities', each team decides what modifications to a fork would be necessary to make it fitter for purpose.

10:15–11:00   Storytelling preparation: 'Unusual Suspects'

Take part in a character-building exercise, so you can tell your story more authentically. You will take turns imagining answers to questions from the serious ('what is your greatest regret?') to the banal ('what is your favourite breakfast?'). Challenge stereotypes and inhabit another person through your imagination, before deploying your character in a matrix game.

11:15–11:30   Matrix game: how to play

Here we will go through the basic rules of a matrix game and take a practice turn together.

11:30–11:45   Morning tea and game planning

11:45–1:15   Matrix game: 'Trouble in the Republic of Arda'

The Republic of Arda is an independent neutral country, consisting of an archipelago in the Eastern sea, with a small Australian embassy. By far, the dominant power in the region is the Hitherlands. In the past, the Republic of Arda has been a treaty ally with the United States but the Hitherlands have made substantial investments in infrastructure. They also have established a growing ethnic Hitherlandian population in the Republic, resulting in growing ethnic tensions and violent protests. An armed militia made up of unmarked fishing vessels has appeared in waters surrounding the Republic of Arda. Australia has decided to evacuate their diplomatic personnel.

Play out a turn-based game designed to flush out problems and inspire innovative solutions for war fighters on the ground.

1:15–1:45   Break for lunch

1:45–3:15   Matrix game: 'Trouble in the Republic of Arda' (continued gameplay)

3:15–3:30   Afternoon tea

3:30–4:15   Get inventive: 'Q's Workshop'

Welcome, Mr Bond. Here in 'Q's Workshop' we come up with all kinds of imaginative ways to solve problems. Imagine you are the genius inventor Q and, drawing on the expertise at your table, see if you can devise some new devices, operations or policy ideas to solve a problem on the list.

4:15–4:45   Debrief, next steps

Our partner from the Business School will discuss the pains and gains you identified over the workshop and lay out the next steps for the collaboration.

5:00–6:00   Drinks and mingle

Future Shock: a two-day scenario-building Story Lab

This collaboration between the University of Queensland's Digital Cultures and Societies Hub and the United Nations High Commissioner for Refugees (UNHCR) was the subject of our case study in Chapter 2. This Story Lab explored the impact of emerging digital technologies on forcefully displaced populations and aimed to anticipate how these technologies would transform the work of the UNHCR and the people it works with in the future. Crucially, the Lab was embedded into a broader programme of activities which lasted close to two weeks, involving public talks and researcher meet-and-greets, all intended to seed the potential for future collaborations.

With this objective in mind, alongside more traditional activities for imagining the future, we incorporated short panel presentations from experts, longer networking lunches and a visit to an art museum on the second day. These longer breaks were welcome as they gave participants who travelled in for the Lab the opportunity to meet and mingle outside of their designated small groups. Participants also reported that the two days of imaginative activities required far more concentration and engagement than a regular conference, and so they welcomed the lighter structure on the second day as it gave them a chance to absorb and reflect on the cross-disciplinary conversations they'd had.

Day 1

9:30–10:10   Welcome

You will be introduced to our creative methodologies while you engage in a short warm-up activity to stimulate your thinking about plausibility and possibility. This exercise will ignite your imagination and help you begin to think about technological convergence in the future.

10:10–10:30   Introduction to the problem

A representative from the UNHCR, our partner organization, will give you a short briefing on the problems they face and the challenges they anticipate in the future.

10:30–10:45   **Morning tea**

10:45–12:45   **Technospaces of forced migration**

This activity uses a deck of cards to help you explore how technologies such as AI, data collection and surveillance, digital identities and predictive analytics are shaping humanitarian responses in the present. You will consider the ethical implications, potential benefits and practical applications of these technologies.

12:45–1:45   **Networking lunch**

1:45–2:30   **Panel presentation**

A panel of experts will present provocative 'snapshots' of the future trajectories of the digital humanitarian problem space, examining geopolitical, ecological and economic domains.

2:30–4:30   **Timelines**

Working in small groups you will map out a timeline of events in five-year increments, which will flesh out potential future trajectories of the world and the technologies that might shape it. You will conclude with short presentations on your scenarios to the whole group.

4:30–5:30   **Drinks and mingle**

Day 2

9:30–10:00   **Coffee and initial reflections**

10:00-10:45   **Welcome to the multiverse**

You will return to the scenarios you created and explore divergence points in your timelines, aiming to come away with one best case scenario, one worst case scenario and one 'weird' scenario.

10:45–11:30   Quantum leap

Members from one group will rotate amongst the other groups, taking on the role of people newly arrived in the world of your scenarios. You will need to explain the rules of this world and how best to survive.

11:30–11:45   Morning tea

11:45–12:30   Developing solutions

In your groups you will think in more detail about what kinds of solutions might be put in place. What is needed? How would it work in practice? The goal is to come up with one pitchable idea, even if it is blue-sky thinking.

12:30–2:30   Lunch off-site and visit to the University of Queensland Art Museum

You will visit the exhibition Mare Amaris, which gathers creative and intellectual practices that dissolve the colonial boundaries of oceans and their connected waters. Wandering on your own or in small groups, find one art piece which speaks to you about the stories you have been telling today. What does it make you feel? What does it make you think of?

2:30–3:45   Solution presentations

Your group will pitch your solutions to the panel as a prompt for discussions about what they reveal about the future, what research directions could be explored and what kinds of collaborations could be useful.

3:45–4:00   Closing remarks

4:00–5:00   Drinks and mingle

8

Victory at the gates: Story Thinking's non-tangible outcomes

Introduction

There is a feeling we sometimes possess (or are possessed by) after finishing a good book: the details of the world sharpen and clarify, greens become greener, blues bluer, our pathways denser with possibility. We find ourselves newly awakened to the sense that underneath, above, beside, beyond the everyday world we inhabit are other possible worlds. In those moments the past and the future do not so much collide as they envelop and overlap. If, as we argued in Chapter 1, stories can hold us in a state of enchantment, then what happens when the story is over? Sometimes this sensation (delicate by its nature) dissipates like a wisp of smoke; other times – if a writer has done their work well – it lingers and continues to act on us. We remain, for some time after, enchanted beings.

The remarkable power of this sensation is difficult to quantify. J. R. R. Tolkien writes, 'The land of fairy-story is wide and deep and high, and is filled with many things … but its very riches and strangeness make dumb the traveller who would report it' (2008: 27). Its fairy gold, he suggests, when brought away, too quickly turns to withered leaves. Science fiction gives us the language of rationality and realism, which is one reason in our guise as researcher-facilitators we tend to adopt it more readily when working with partners from other disciplines. Yet when it comes time to articulate the value of the Story Thinking we often find the grammar of fantasy more capable, precisely because it is better accustomed to expressing the intangible.

Slipping out of the language of fantasy, edging closer toward that of the researcher-artist, we follow Graeme Sullivan in suggesting that knowledge is not always generated through data collection and analysis. Rather, knowledge can also be revealed through a dynamic process of interaction and reflection between artists, the artworks and their audiences. Sullivan argues that 'these forms of understanding are grounded in human experiences and interactions and yield outcomes that can be individually liberating and culturally enlightening' (2010: 97). Here we find resonance with the work of the futurist Marcus Bussey (2016; 2017) who suggests that one's framing of the future depends on five cultural senses: memory, voice, yearning, optimism and foresight: 'We remember and anticipate (memory and foresight). We act as if we were for the most part free agents (voice). We cherish hopes for the future (optimism) and we yearn for greater meaning, greater fulfilment, more belonging or simply more (yearning)' (Bussey 2017: 50). Together these form an anticipatory aesthetics that can invite an 'adventure into possibility' (ibid.) and address 'the human compulsion to "make sense of" by ordering, classifying, harmonising and explaining' (ibid.: 57). We draw on Bussey here because we see shared space between his conception of the role of aesthetics in futures studies and Sullivan's practice-oriented framing of research outcomes. In writing this book, we have quested after ways to secure for the Humanities a seat at the transdisciplinary table, at a time when traditional

Humanities disciplines, especially the arts, are undergoing challenge and change. But in doing so we also find it pragmatic and essential to articulate our contribution in terms that speak to our own values and disciplinary practices.

But we recognize that often, particularly as we seek common ground with other disciplines, it isn't enough to speak to altered qualities of emotion and perception, however valuable we might find them as ends unto themselves. The historical bent of futures studies has striven to link foresight processes 'directly to decision and action' (Stevenson 2001: 669). Underlying this is an assumption common in the discipline that a scenario project has failed if you haven't changed something in the mind of managers (Wack 1985) and that the work has been a waste unless something tangible happens (Burt and van der Heijden 2003). We notice a similar impulse in participatory design studies. Whittle (2014) argues the early phases of scholarship focused on tangible results for users, whereas the recent trend has been toward seeing research papers as the best outcomes. We note that he too classifies outcomes as tangible deliverables such as follow-on funding bids, digital prototypes, and written documents. Although he recognizes the importance of intangible benefits such as up-skilling or confidence building, he finds them 'much harder to measure' although he does admit 'they are one of the strongest benefits' (2014: 124). His study of six participatory design projects concludes by arguing against too much focus on a single outcome (e.g. the product that is to be designed) which risks ignoring many other outcomes. We understand and find some solidarity with the self-consciousness here, the impatience with disciplines building their research base, given we ourselves are so often asked to frame the value of creative writing in the most instrumental terms. But in this conclusion we want to hold space for the full range of outcomes, tangible and intangible.

Some of the negotiated 'deliverables' of the case studies we have discussed in this book include workshop models, methodological papers, conference presentations, scenario fragments as well as fully fleshed-out scenarios, partner-led analysis intended for strategic planners, government reports, planned funding bids, partnerships and network building, teaching materials, positive course evaluations, participant up-skilling, capacity building, incorporation of exercises into training documentation, creative artefacts ranging from narrative scenarios to bespoke board games, innovation prompts, positive workshop experiences as indicated via feedback forms, knowledge transfer via facilitator handbooks and training, organizational risk mitigation, joy, a community of practice, improved pipelines for research collaborations, incremental changes in organizational culture, lasting friendships and re-energized commitments to our own disciplines. Some of these deliverables have been measurable but others, as Whittle observes, are much harder to quantify.

We've divided this book into two sections: the first four chapters present Story Thinking's conceptual framework and introduce our four domains (Inhabit; Envision; Empathize; Engage); while the final three focus on putting these ideas into practice. We acknowledge that the work of Story Thinking can be strengthened by planning for tangible outcomes, translated into a context and form that makes sense for our partners and collaborators, but we don't want to too easily abandon the intangibles that make our work valuable. As a result we draw attention to four specific themes below:

Building creative capacity

Story Thinking naturally strengthens practitioners' narrative cognition: their ability to understand diverse contexts, to think causally, to adopt new perspectives and to wield language effectively to generate possibilities and make meaning. Fletcher and Benveniste (2022) argue convincingly that approaches to building creative capacity grounded in narrative cognition are already yielding promising results, particularly in situations where the data for accurate calculation or computation are often missing (which we would argue is the case for most complex problems, by their nature). They find AI 'extremely fragile in unstable and uncertain environments' (2022: 33) where it struggles to generate and refine original actions in response to new challenges or opportunities. Given the scale of the challenges our society faces, we argue – and the evidence across fields suggests – that the ability to solve problems creatively will continue to be important.

Moreover, as should be apparent from the Dungeon Master's Guide, Story Thinking encourages playfulness. Play is heavily associated with childhood, and for that reason some people think of it as something we have to grow out of, something that's trivial or worthless, and this idea is well and truly ingrained before we reach the workplace. In fact, play and work are often seen as opposites of each other. A study by the National Institute for Play in the United States looked at the habits of 6,000 people and concluded play led to brain plasticity, adaptability and creativity. The lead researcher, Stuart Brown, writes that play 'shapes the brain and makes animals smarter and more adaptable' (Brown and Vaughan 2010: 12). Neuroscientist Jaak Panskepp describes play as highly beneficial for the brain, 'including the facilitation of certain types of learning' and allowing mammals 'to be effectively assimilated into the structures of their society' (2004: 280). The double gift of play is that it is both fun (for exploring and imagining) and has been proven to improve executive function: psychiatrist Edward Hallowell shows play's positive effect on planning, prioritizing, anticipating, decision-making and analysis (2011: 125).

We often describe the benefits of Story Thinking to building creative capacity as follows: every human has an imagination; it is software installed at birth. Many people, however, haven't updated their software since primary school. Story Thinking can provide a much-needed software update.

Understanding systems and how they change

Stories help us navigate complexity, granting powerful insights into how existing systems are formed and how they may change. Crucially, they also present the possibility of startling newness: future worlds, adjacent worlds, undiscovered worlds, all of which might help researchers understand their problem spaces. Story Thinking offers an effective way to situate, map and un-silo specialized knowledge. As Lombardo argues, sensory detail, nuance and drama – all important characteristics of science fiction and fantasy – work together to create stories that are more compelling and realistic 'than an abstract futurist scenario or statistical prediction' (2018: 2) because they embody 'a fully realized, multidimensional vision, including not only the technological and scientific, but the psychological, cultural, moral, social, and environmental dimensions of future human existence' (ibid.: 3). Thinking through stories forces researchers to move beyond discrete areas of knowledge to see how all the pieces of the system work together to determine outcomes.

Story Thinking also helps researchers to acknowledge the truth that systems change as a result of the agency of individuals as well as broader societal or environmental forces, which must be navigated rather than controlled. Understanding a story as a system – interdependent parts interacting over time – allows us to 'storify' problems. Drop them into the Story Thinking model and use those readily understood concepts of plot, setting and character to understand the problem better, move towards defining it more clearly and try out possibilities for solutions. Zoom in on a particular character individually, or zoom out to an organization or population level. Switch settings and see how the complexion of the problem changes. Add complications or remove them, and speculate on what would happen in the system. Story Thinking provides a way to imagine, reimagine and reframe complex problems as they evolve.

Reducing future shock

The pace of technological and social change can leave researchers feeling disoriented and anxious, a state encapsulated by Alvin Toffler's famous term 'future shock' (1970). We ourselves have felt this in our research trajectories as the institutions we have worked in have shifted incrementally in response to demographics and market conditions as well as through sudden accelerations or swift changes necessitating immediate responses (organizational restructures to the Brexit referendum's immediate impact on research funding through to Covid-19 and the advent of generative AI, to name a few). When researchers become aware of a shift in their environment such that it no longer matches their expectations, they can have difficulty adjusting. But one way to reframe this is by thinking about how readers, or indeed Story Thinkers more generally, immerse themselves in new fictional worlds. Readers often find it easier at first to engage with realistic fiction because their cognitive frames are still largely relevant for interpreting the story while in the case of 'fantastic or futuristic' fiction, readers need to work harder to 'construct a mental image' (Ryan and Thon 2014: 3) that can function as a world-like proxy. After a 'painful period of initiation' (Ryan 2015: 13), however, they are able to instantly immerse into new worlds, to instantly see them as world-like instead of being something strange and remote. Story Thinking's practice of imagining alternate or counterfactual worlds can prepare researchers for periods of accelerated change, helping them to shrink the period of disorientation. Lest this seem too woolly, Major General Mick Ryan points out that in this 'age of acceleration' there exists a capability gap in military organizations, which can result from 'a failure in imagination, a failure of anticipation and a failure of adaptation' (2019: 24). He founded the Perry Group within the Australian Defence College, an elective course we have taught into, which takes science fiction as a framework, asking students to write short papers (some traditional, some with integrated narrative scenarios) for senior leaders in Defence on future challenges. The point here? Imagining alternative worlds can help us react swiftly when the world around us changes.

Enhancing collaborative research cultures

Threaded through this book has been a focus on how to build better collaborations by drawing on the strengths of diversity, by sparking passionate engagement and creating safe spaces for risk-taking and creativity. In saying that, we recognize that research collaborations are necessarily fluid: roles shift, partners leave, join, become distracted, change their focus and levels of investment. Institutional structures may provide a sense of continuity but crucially so does shared culture. Our sense of a research culture goes beyond the organizational culture that shapes research collaborations to incorporate 'ways of life' or shared meanings and 'special processes of discovery and creativity' (Williams [1958] 1989: 4) as well as the shared interest in conduct that artist Kate Foster and cultural geographer Hayden Lorimer argue can matter as much as a shared vision for content (2007: 427). Supporting and enhancing that sense of shared culture ought to be an outcome in and of itself. This draws together several themes in creative arts research more generally: a shift from creative outputs to the collaborative process of working together and a growing recognition of collaboration itself as an arts-based 'form of enquiry' (Ward and Shortt 2020: 2).

Happily ever after?

'I believe in the power of the imagination to remake the world,' wrote J. G. Ballard in his visionary manifesto for his own writing, 'to release the truth within us, to hold back the night, to transcend death, to charm motorways, to ingratiate ourselves with birds, to enlist the confidences of madmen' (1984). Deep inside we three authors is a desire to pin this to the doorway of every scientist, doctor and engineer of every university we walk through as a call to action, our own invitation to adventure into possibility.

We can all be artists. If we are to do anything worthwhile, we all *must* be artists. The world demands no less of us.

We three began this work because we are naturally curious; we find ourselves easily enchanted by the research fields of others, by charismatic megastructures – bridges, railways and power plants – and the alien language of calculus and quantum mechanics. At heart we are the children who forgot the warnings of the fairy tale: do not stray from the path. We ignored the warnings of our grandmothers: be bold, be bold, but not too bold. We recognize now is the moment for boldness. Besides, we have always been happier lost in the deep forest, with its mysterious strangers, hidden pathways, dangers, adventure and joy – or on the high mountain where the air seems to fizz on our tongues, where the light takes on the quality of ether.

For it is there we can look at the stars and wonder, 'What if?'

We can look to each other and ask, 'What else?'

We can look to our work and ask, 'What for?'

These are the questions we leave you with, weary traveller – our ingots of gold. We have come by them honestly and we give them willingly for you have quested for some time with us. Ah – we understand your hesitation. Haven't we just said the stuff of fairy-land is tricksy and impermanent? Haven't we warned that in a moment, when you close the pages of this book, all you will be left with is withered leaves? You fear a cheat. But if you have learned our lore then you know there is another way …

Not all adventurers leave the forest. Some choose enchantment.

We hope you do.

BIBLIOGRAPHY

Adams, J. (1989), 'Causality and Narrative', *Journal of Literary Semantics*, 18 (3): 149–62.

Adams, K. M. (2011), 'Systems Principles: Foundation for the SoSE Methodology', *International Journal of System of Systems Engineering*, 2 (2): 120–55.

Adams, T. E., Jones, S. H. and C. Ellis (2014), *Autoethnography*, Oxford: Oxford University Press.

Ainsworth, S. E. and K. Scheiter (2021), 'Learning by Drawing Visual Representations: Potential, Purposes, and Practical Implications', *Current Directions in Psychological Science*, 30 (1): 61–7.

Alderman, N. (2016), *The Power*, New York: Viking.

Alfonso, M. R. A., Lagmay, A. M. S., Atayde, J. A., Bautista, K. and M. I. Lukban (2022), 'A/r/tography, Rhizomatic Storytelling, and Ripple Effects Mapping: A Combined Arts-Based and Community Mapping Methodology to Evaluate the Impact of COVID-19 Expressive Arts Support Groups for Frontliners in the Philippines', in E. Bos and E. Huss (eds), *Social Work Research Using Arts-Based Methods*, 148–61, Bristol: Bristol University Press.

Amis, M. (1991), *Time's Arrow*, London: Jonathan Cape.

Andersen, D., Ravn, S. and R. Thomson (2020), 'Narrative Sense-Making and Prospective Social Action: Methodological Challenges and New Directions', *International Journal of Social Research Methodology*, 23 (4): 367–75.

Andersson, J. (2018), *The Future of the World: Futurology, Futurists, and the Struggle for the Post-Cold War Imagination*, Oxford: Oxford University Press.

Anderton, J., Ivanova, K., Marshall, H., Wilkins, K., Bennett, L. and H. Scott (2023), 'Web 3.0 Technology Impacts and Future Scenarios', Canberra: Human and Decision Sciences Division, Defence Science Technology Group.

Anzaldúa, G. (2015), *Light in the Dark/Luz En Lo Oscuro: Rewriting Identity, Spirituality, Reality*, bilingual edn, edited by A.-L. Keating, Durham: Duke University Press.

Atwood, M. (1985), *The Handmaid's Tale*, Toronto: McClelland and Stewart Houghton.

Awati, R., Bernstein, C. and I. Wigmore (2022), 'Moonshot', *TechTarget*, May. Available online: https://www.techtarget.com/whatis/definition/moonshot (Accessed: 12 October 2023).

Awdish, R. (2018), *In Shock: How Nearly Dying Made Me a Better Intensive Care Doctor*, New York: Bantam.

Bailey, D. (1992), *J. R. R. Tolkien: A Study of John Ronald Reuel Tolkien 1892–1973*, [Film] UK: Films for the Humanities & Sciences, 1 January.

Ballard, J. G. (1984), 'What I Believe', *Interzone*, #8, originally published in French in D. Richie (ed.), *Science Fiction #1*, 1–4. Reproduced and available online: http://www.jgballard.ca/uncollected_work/what_i_believe.html (Accessed: 15 September 2023).

Barnett, A. and Z. Doubleday (2020), 'Meta-Research: The Growth of Acronyms in the Scientific Literature', *eLife*, 9:e60080: 1–10.

Beach, L. R. (2009), 'Decision Making: Linking Narratives and Action', *Narrative Inquiry*, 19 (2): 393–414.

Bear, E. (2022), Interviewed by Joanne Anderston, 9 September, Zoom.

Bell, W. (2005), 'Creativity, Skepticism, and Visioning the Future', *Futures*, 37 (5): 429–32.

Belton, O. and S. Dillon (2021), 'Futures of Autonomous Flight: Using a Collaborative Storytelling Game to Assess Anticipatory Assumptions', *Futures*, 128: 1–13.

Bleecker, J. (2009), 'Design Fiction: A Short Essay on Design, Science, Fact and Fiction'. Available online: https://systemsorienteddesign.net/wp-content/uploads/2011/01/DesignFiction_WebEdition.pdf (Accessed: 4 December 2023).

Bode, C. and R. Dietrich (2013), *Future Narratives: Theory, Poetics, and Media-Historical Moment*, Berlin: W. de Gruyter.

Boyd, B. (2009), *On the Origin of Stories: Evolution, Cognition, and Fiction*, Cambridge, MA: The Belknap Press of Harvard University Press.

Bracken, L. J. and E. A. Oughton (2006), '"What Do You Mean?" The Importance of Language in Developing Interdisciplinary Research', *Transactions of the Institute of British Geographers*, 31 (3): 371–82.

Bradbury, R. (1992), *Zen in the Art of Writing*, New York: Bantam.

Bridgland, V. M. E., Barnard, J. F. and M. K. T. Takarangi (2022), 'Unprepared: Thinking of a Trigger Warning Does Not Prompt Preparation for Trauma-Related Content', *Journal of Behavior Therapy and Experimental Psychiatry*, 75 (101708): 1–8.

brown, adrienne mareeadarad and W. Imarisha (2015), *Octavia's Brood: Science Fiction Stories from Social Justice Movements*, Oakland: Ak Press.

Brown, A. and E. Weiner (1985), *Supermanaging: How to Harness Change for Personal and Organizational Success*, New York: Mentor.

Brown, S. and C. Vaughan (2010), *Play: How It Shapes the Brain, Opens the Imagination, and Invigorates the Soul*, Melbourne: Scribe Publications.

Brown, T. (2008), 'Design Thinking', *Harvard Business Review*, June. Available online: https://hbr.org/2008/06/design-thinking (Accessed: 18 March 2023).

Burt, G. and K. van der Heijden (2003), 'First Steps: Towards Purposeful Activities in Scenario Thinking and Future Studies', *Futures* 35 (10): 1011–26.

Bussey, M. (2016), 'The Hidden Curriculum of Futures Studies: Introducing the Futures Senses', *World Futures Review*, 8 (1): 39–45.

Bussey, M. (2017), 'Anticipatory Aesthetics: New Identities and Future Senses', in J. Clammer and A. K. Giri (eds), *The Aesthetics of Development: Art, Culture and Social Transformation*, 49–70, London: Palgrave Macmillan.

Campbell, J. (1949), *The Hero with a Thousand Faces*, New York: Pantheon Books.

Carr, M. (2010), 'Slouching towards Dystopia: The New Military Futurism,' *Race & Class*, 51 (3): 13–32.

Carter, A. ([1979] 2006), *The Bloody Chamber and Other Stories*. London: Vintage Books.

Carter, A. J., Croft, A., Lukas, D. and G. M. Sandstrom (2018), 'Women's Visibility in Academic Seminars: Women Ask Fewer Questions than Men', *PLOS ONE*, 13 (9): 1–22.

Castillo, M. (2009), 'Futurism and Scientific Networking', *American Journal of Neuroradiology*, 2 April. Available online: https://doi.org/10.3174/ajnr.A1582 (Accessed: 5 April 2023).

Chatman, S. (1978), *Story and Discourse: Narrative Structure in Fiction and Film, Story and Discourse*, New York: Cornell University Press.

Chlopczyk, J. and C. Erlach (2019), 'The Narrative Approach to Transforming Organizations', in J. Chlopczyk and C. Erlach (eds), *Transforming Organizations: Narrative and Story-Based Approaches*, 1–8, Cham: Springer International Publishing.

Cooney, C. S. E. and C. Hernandez (2022), Interviewed by Lisa Bennett. 29 April, Zoom.

Cowen, V. S., Kaufman, D. and L. Schoenherr (2016), 'A Review of Creative and Expressive Writing as a Pedagogical Tool in Medical Education', *Medical Education*, 50 (3): 311–19.

Cron, L. (2012), *Wired for Story: The Writer's Guide to Using Brain Science to Hook Readers From the Very First Sentence*, Berkeley: Ten Speed Press.

Curry, J., Price, T. and T. Mouat (2023), *Advanced Matrix Games for Professional Wargaming: Innovations in Wargaming*, Independently published.

Curwood, J. S. (2013), 'Fan Fiction, Remix Culture, and The Potter Games', in V. E. Frankel (ed.), *Teaching with Harry Potter*, 81–92, Jefferson: McFarland.

Delany, S. R. (2013), *About Writing: Seven Essays, Four Letters, & Five Interviews*, Middletown: Wesleyan University Press.

Dellamonica, A. and K. Robson (2022), Interviewed by Lisa Bennett. 10 May, Zoom.

Dillon, S. and C. Craig (2022), *Storylistening: Narrative Evidence and Public Reasoning*, Abingdon: Routledge.

Dinar, M., Shah, J., Langley, P., Hunt, G. and E. Campana (2011), 'A Structure for Representing Problem Formulation in Design', *ICED 11 – 18th International Conference on Engineering Design – Impacting Society Through Engineering Design, vol. 6: Design Information and Knowledge*, 392–401.

Doty, W. G. (2014), *Mythography: The Study of Myths and Rituals*, 1st edn, Tuscaloosa: The University of Alabama Press.

Douglas, K. (2024), '"Not Another ARC Summer": Grant Applications and Life Narratives of Motherhood', in L. Ortiz-Vilarelle (ed.), *Career Narratives and Academic Womanhood: In the Spaces Provided*, 100–14, Abingdon: Routledge, Taylor & Francis.

Edelenbos, J., Bressers, N. and L. Vandenbussche (2017), 'Evolution of Interdisciplinary Collaboration: What are Stimulating Conditions?', *Science and Public Policy*, 44 (4): 451–63.

Fergnani, A. (2019), 'The Future Persona: A Futures Method to Let your Scenarios Come to Life', *Foresight*, 21 (4): 445–66.

Finn, E. and R. Wylie (2021), 'Collaborative Imagination: A Methodological Approach', *Futures*, 132. Available online: https://doi.org/10.1016/j.futures.2021.102788 (Accessed: 14 January 2023).

Fischer, N. and W. Mehnert (2021), 'Building Possible Worlds: A Speculation Based Framework to Reflect on Images of the Future', *Journal of Futures Studies*, 25 (3): 25–38.

Fischer, T. (2017), 'Spaceman of Bohemia by Jaroslav Kalfar Review – Solaris with Laughs', *The Guardian*, 17 March. Available online: https://www.theguardian.com/books/2017/

mar/17/spaceman-of-bohemia-by-jaroslav-kalfar-review (Accessed: 4 November 2023).

Fitzgerald, F. S. (1950), *The Great Gatsby*, New York: Penguin Books.

Fletcher, A. and M. Benveniste (2022), 'A New Method for Training Creativity: Narrative as an Alternative to Divergent Thinking', *Annals of the New York Academy of Sciences*, 1512 (1): 29–45.

Flood, A. (2011), 'Getting More from George RR Martin', *The Guardian*, 14 April. Available online: https://www.theguardian.com/books/booksblog/2011/apr/14/more-george-r-r-martin (Accessed: 12 April 2023).

Forster, E. M. (1927), *Aspects of the Novel*, London: Edward Arnold.

Foster, K. and H. Lorimer (2007), 'Cultural Geographies in Practice: Some Reflections on Art-Geography as Collaboration', *Cultural Geographies*, 14 (3): 425–32.

Frey, J. N. (2010), *How to Write a Damn Good Novel*, New York: St Martin's Press.

Friess, E. (2012), 'Personas and Decision Making in the Design Process: An Ethnographic Case Study', *Proceedings of the SIGCHI Conference on Human Factors in Computing Systems*: 1209–18.

Gee, J. P. (2005), 'Semiotic Social Spaces and Affinity Spaces: From the Age of Mythology to Today's Schools', in D. Barton and K. Tusting (eds), *Beyond Communities of Practice: Language, Power, and Social Context*, 214–32, New York: Cambridge University Press.

Gibson, R., Crea, T. and G. Chambers (2018), 'Narration and Dramaturgy in Emergency Situations', *Axon: Creative Explorations*, 8 (2). Available online: https://axonjournal.com.au/issues/8-2/narration-and-dramaturgy-emergency-situations (Accessed: 4 December 2023).

Gibson, W. (1984), *Neuromancer*. New York: Ace.

Gibson, W. (1986), *Burning Chrome*, New York: HarperCollins.

Gilligan, J. M. (2019), 'Expertise Across Disciplines: Establishing Common Ground in Interdisciplinary Disaster Research Teams', *Risk Analysis*, 41 (7): 1171–7.

Glăveanu, V. P. (2014) *Distributed Creativity: Thinking Outside the Box of the Creative Individual*, Cham: Springer.

Glăveanu, V. P. and L. Tanggaard (2014), 'Creativity, Identity, and Representation: Towards a Socio-cultural Theory of Creative Identity', *New Ideas in Psychology*, 34: 12–21.

Gottschall, J. (2012), *The Storytelling Animal: How Stories Make Us Human*, Boston: Houghton Mifflin Harcourt.

Grady, S. M., Schmälzle R. and J. Baldwin (2022), 'Examining the Relationship between Story Structure and Audience Response: How Shared Brain Activity Varies over the Course of a Narrative', *Projections*, 16 (3): 1–28.

Gray, J. (2003), 'New Audiences, New Textualities: Anti-Fans and Non-Fans', *International Journal of Cultural Studies*, 6 (1): 64–81.

Green, D. (2016), *How Change Happens*, Oxford: Oxford University Press.

Green, M. C. and T. C. Brock (2000), 'The Role of Transportation in the Persuasiveness of Public Narratives', *Journal of Personality and Social Psychology*, 79: 701–21.

Gross, P. (2010), 'Small Worlds: What Works in Workshops If and When They Do?', in D. Donnelly (ed.), *Does the Writing Workshop Still Work?*, 52–62, Bristol; Blue Ridge Summit: Multilingual Matters.

Gygax, G. (1979), *The Keep on the Borderlands: Dungeon Module B2*, Lake Geneva: TSR Games.

Hagberg, G. L. (2013), 'Ensemble Improvisation, Collective Intention, and Group Attention', in Lewis, G. E. and B. Piekut (eds), *The Oxford Handbook of Critical Improvisation Studies, Volume 1*, 481–99, Oxford: Oxford Academic.

Hagtvedt, L. P., Dossinger, K., Harrison, S. H. and L. Huang (2019) 'Curiosity Made the Cat More Creative: Specific Curiosity as a Driver of Creativity', *Organizational Behavior and Human Decision Processes*, 150: 1–13.

Hallowell, E. (2011), *Shine: Using Brain Science to Get the Best from Your People*, Brighton: Harvard Business Press.

Hamalian, L. (1970), 'The Visible Voice: An Approach to Writing', *The English Journal*, 59 (2): 227–30.

Hardy, R. D. (2018), 'A Sharing Meanings Approach for Interdisciplinary Hazards Research', *Risk Analysis*, 41 (7): 1162–70.

Harkaway, N. (2021), 'Envision', Paper presented at the What If Consortium, Workshop 1, 23 July.

Harper, J. (2017), *Blades in the Dark*, Evil Hat Productions.

Harris, R. (1992), *Fatherland*, London: Hutchinson.

Harrison, M. J. (1975), 'Sweet Analytics', in H. Bailey (ed.) *New Worlds 9*, London: Corgi.

Harrison, M. J. (1989), 'The Profession of Science Fiction, 40: The Profession of Fiction', in *Foundation*, Fall 1989, 5–13. Available at: https://www.proquest.com/docview/1312025485/fulltext/C01B85C722034E21PQ/1?accountid=8318&imgSeq=1 (Accessed: 12 April 2023).

Harrison, M. J. (2001), 'What it Might Be Like to Live in Viriconium', Fantastic Metropolis. Available at: https://fantasticmetropolis.com/i/viriconium (Accessed: 21 April 2023).

Harrison, M. J. (2007), 'Very Afraid', *Uncle Zip's Window*, 27 January. Available online: https://web.archive.org/web/20080205000327/http://uzwi.wordpress.com/2007/01/27/very-afraid/ (Accessed: 23 October 2019).

Hartley, N. (2007), 'Creativity and Resilience', in B. Monroe and D. Oliviere (eds), *Resilience in Palliative Care: Achievement in Adversity*, 281–92, Oxford: Oxford University Press.

Headley, M. D. (2021), *Beowulf: A New Translation*. London: Scribe.

Hellekson, K. (2009), 'Alternative History', in Mark Bould, Andrew M. Butler, Adam Roberts and Sherryl Vint (eds), *The Routledge Companion to Science Fiction*, Abingdon: Routledge, 453–7.

Hildebrandt, M. (2021), 'Creativity and Resilience in Art Students During COVID-19', *Art Education*, 74 (1): 17–18.

Ho, C.-h. (2001), 'Some Phenomena of Problem Decomposition Strategy for Design Thinking: Differences Between Novices and Experts', *Design Studies*, 22 (1): 27–45.

Huang, L., Gino, F. and A. D. Galinsky (2015), 'The Highest Form of Intelligence: Sarcasm Increases Creativity for Both Expressers and Recipients', *Organizational Behavior and Human Decision Processes*, 131: 162–77.

Huizinga, J. (1995), *Homo Ludens: A Study of the Play Element in Culture*. Boston: The Beacon Press.

Huotilainen, M., Rankanen, M., Growth, C., Seitamaa-hakkarainen, P. and M. Mäkelä (2018) 'Why Our Brains Love Arts and Crafts: Implications of Creative Practices on Psychophysical Well-being', *FormAkademisk*, 11 (2): 1–18.

Iser, W. (1980), *The Act of Reading: A Theory of Aesthetic Response*, Baltimore: Johns Hopkins University Press.

Ivanova, K., Elsawah, S. and J. Fidock (2020), 'Technological Ecosystems in Capability Development: A Case Study in Emerging Technologies', *Systems Engineering*, 23 (4): 423–35.

Jackson, M. C. (2019), *Critical Systems Thinking and the Management of Complexity*, Hoboken and Chichester: John Wiley & Sons.

Jacob, F. (1998), *Of Flies, Mice and Men*, Cambridge, MA: Harvard University Press.

Jansen, B. J., Salminen, J. O., and S. Jung (2020), 'Data-Driven Personas for Enhanced User Understanding: Combining Empathy with Rationality for Better Insights to Analytics', *Data and Information Management*, 4 (1): 1–17.

Jarva, V. (2014), 'Introduction to Narrative for Futures Studies', *Journal of Futures Studies*, 18 (3): 5–26.

Jemisin, N. K. (2014), 'Why I Talk So Damn Much About Non-Writing Stuff', *NK Jemisin*, 13 October. Available online: http://nkjemisin.com/2014/10/why-i-talk-so-damn-much-about-non-writing-stuff/ (Accessed: 23 September 2020).

Jemisin, N. K. (2015–2017), *The Broken Earth* series. 3 vols. London: Little, Brown.

Jemisin, N. K. (2018), 'N. K. Jemisin's 2018 Hugo Award Best Novel acceptance speech', *YouTube*, 20 August. Available online: https://www.youtube.com/watch?v=8lFybhRxoVM (Accessed: 4 October 2023).

Jenkins, H. (2006), *Convergence Culture: Where Old and New Media Collide*, New York: NYU Press.

Jeong, S. and J. Y. Choi (2015), 'Collaborative Research for Academic Knowledge Creation: How Team Characteristics, Motivation, and Processes Influence Research Impact', *Science and Public Policy*, 42: 460–73.

Johnson, B. D. (2011), *Science Fiction Prototyping: Designing the Future with Science Fiction*, Kentfield: Morgan & Claypool.

Johnson, M. (2013), *Family, Village, Tribe: The Evolution of Flight Centre*, William Heinemann Australia.

Johnson, S. (2010), *Where Good Ideas Come From: The Natural History of Innovation*, London: Allen Lane.

Jones, P. J., Bellet, B. W. and R. J. McNally (2020), 'Helping or Harming? The Effect of Trigger Warnings on Individuals with Trauma Histories', *Clinical Psychological Science*, 8 (5): 905–17.

Jones, T. (2012), *Poetic Language: Theory and Practice from the Renaissance to the Present.* Edinburgh: Edinburgh University Press.

Kalfař, J. (2017), *Spaceman of Bohemia.* London: Hachette UK.

Kauffman, S. A. (2000), *Investigations*, Oxford: Oxford University Press.

Kayılı, G. and Z. Erdal (2021), 'Children's Problem Solving Skills: Does Drama Based Storytelling Method Work?', *Journal of Childhood, Education & Society*, 2 (1): 43–57.

Keller, C. (1986), *From a Broken Web: Separation, Sexism, and Self*, Boston: Beacon Press.

Kelley, T. (2005), *The Ten Faces of Innovation*, New York: Random House.

Kercheval, J. L. (2003), *Building Fiction: How to Develop Plot and Structure*, Wisconsin: University of Wisconsin Press.

King, S., as R. Bachman (1979), *The Long Walk*, New York: Signet Books.

Kirby, D. (2010), 'The Future is Now: Diegetic Prototypes and the Role of Popular Films in Generating Real-World Technological Development', *Social Studies of Science*, 40 (1): 41–70.

Klein, G. (2007), 'Performing a Project Premortem', *Harvard Business Review*, September. Available online: https://hbr.org/2007/09/performing-a-project-premortem (Accessed: 2 January 2022).

Klein, J. (1990), *Interdisciplinarity: History, Theory, and Practice*. Detroit: Wayne State University Press.

Kok, K. P. W., Gjefsen, M. D., Regeer, B. J. and J. E. W. Broerse (2021), 'Unraveling the Politics of "Doing Inclusion" in Transdisciplinarity for Sustainable Transformation', *Sustainability Science*, 16 (6): 1811–26.

Kotecha, M. C., Chen, T.-J., McAdams, D. A. and V. Krishnamurthy (2021), 'Design Ideation Through Speculative Fiction: Foundational Principles and Exploratory Study', *Journal of Mechanical Design*, 143 (8): 1–16.

Kress, N. (1993), *Beggars in Spain*. New York: William Morrow.

Kushner, E. and D. Sherman (2022), Interviewed by Lisa Bennett. 3 May, Zoom.

Lammers, J. C., Curwood, J. S. and A. M. Magnifico (2012), 'Toward an Affinity Space Methodology: Considerations for Literacy Research', *English Teaching: Practice and Critique*, 11 (2): 44–58.

Lankshear, C. and M. Knobel (2007), 'Researching New Literacies: Web 2.0 Practices and Insider Perspectives', *E-Learning and Digital Media*, 4 (3): 224–40.

Le Guin, U. K. (1968), *A Wizard of Earthsea*, New York and London: Bantam.

Le Guin, U. K. (2017), *The Ones Who Walk Away from Omelas*, New York: Harper Perennial.

Leifer, L. and C. Meinel (2018), 'Looking Further: Design Thinking Beyond Solution-Fixation', in C. Meinel and L. Leifer (eds), *Design Thinking Research: Understanding Innovation*, 1–12, Cham: Springer.

Leppänen, S. (2009), 'Playing with and Policing Language Use and Textuality in Fan Fiction', in I. Hotz-Davies, A. Kirchhofer and S. Leppänen (eds), *Internet Fictions*, 62–83, Newcastle upon Tyne: Cambridge Scholars Publishing.

Liveley, G., Slocombe, W. and E. Spiers (2021), 'Futures Literacy through Narrative,' *Futures*, 125: 1–9.

Lombardo, T. (2018), *Science Fiction: The Evolutionary Mythology of the Future*, vol. 1, Alresford: Changemakers Books.

Mandala, S. (2010), *The Language in Science Fiction and Fantasy: The Question of Style*, London: Continuum.

Mar, R. A. and K. Oatley (2008), 'The Function of Fiction is the Abstraction and Simulation of Social Experience', *Perspectives on Psychological Science: A Journal of the Association for Psychological Science*, 3 (3): 173–92.

Marshall, H. (2019), *The Migration*, London: Titan Books.

Marshall, H., Jennings, K. and J. Anderton (2023), 'Science Fiction for Hire? Notes towards an Emerging Practice of Creative Futurism', *TEXT*, 27 (2). Available online: https://doi.org/10.52086/001c.89087 (Accessed: 4 December 2023).

Marshall, H., Wilkins, K., Bennett, L., Ivanova, K. and J. Anderton (2023), 'Support, Structure and Speed: Key Concepts for the Digital Delivery of Creative Foresight Workshops', *Journal of Futures Studies*. In press. Available online: https://jfsdigital. org/support-structure-and-speed-key-concepts-for-the-digital-delivery-of-creative-foresight-workshops/

Marshall, T. (2016), *Prisoners of Geography: Ten Maps That Tell You Everything You Need to Know About Global Politics*, London: Elliott & Thompson.

Masini, E. (1993), *Why Futures Studies?*, London: Grey Seal.

McGonigal, J. (2010), 'Gaming Can Make a Better World', *TED*, February. Available online: https://www.ted.com/talks/jane_mcgonigal_gaming_can_make_a_better_world (Accessed: 20 December 2021).

McGreavy, B., Haynal, K., Smith-Mayo, J., Reilly-Moman, J., Kinnison, M. T., Ranco, D. and H. M. Leslie (2022), 'How Does Strategic Communication Shape Transdisciplinary Collaboration? A Focus on Definitions, Audience, Expertise, and Ethical Praxis', *Frontiers in Communication*, 7: 1–14.

McKee, R. (1999), *Story: Substance, Structure, Style, and the Principles of Screenwriting*, London: Methuen.

Meltzoff, A. N. (2010), 'Social Cognition and the Origins of Imitation, Empathy, and Theory of Mind', in U. Goswami (ed.), *The Wiley-Blackwell Handbook of Childhood Cognitive Development*, 49–75, New York: John Wiley & Sons.

Metzl, E. S. (2009), 'The Role of Creative Thinking in Resilience after Hurricane Katrina', *Psychology of Aesthetics, Creativity, and the Arts*, 3 (2): 112–23.

Milburn, C. (2008), *Nanovision: Engineering the Future*, Durham: Duke University Press.

Miles, I. (1993), 'Stranger than Fiction: How Important is Science Fiction for Futures Studies?', *Futures*, 25 (3): 315–21.

Montola, M. (2010), 'The Positive Negative Experience in Extreme Role-Playing', *DiGRA Nordic '10: Proceedings of the 2010 International DiGRA Nordic Conference: Experiencing Games: Games, Play, and Players*, vol. 9.

More, E., Probert, D. and R. Phaal (2015), 'Improving Long-Term Strategic Planning: An Analysis of STEEPLE Factors Identified in Environmental Scanning Brainstorms', *2015 Portland International Conference on Management of Engineering and Technology (PICMET)*: 381–94. Available online: https://doi.org/10.1109/PICMET.2015.7273126 (Accessed: 4 December 2023).

Morris, J. and R. G. Van Cleave. (2021), 'The Truth About Plot', *The Writer*, 134 (7): 18–21.

Nelson, R. (2013), *Practice as Research in the Arts: Principles, Protocols, Pedagogies, Resistances*, London: Palgrave.

Newell, A. and H. A. Simon (1972), *Human Problem Solving*, Englewood Cliffs: Prentice-Hall.

Nicholson, S. (2010), 'The Problem of Woman as Hero in the Work of Joseph Campbell', *Feminist Theology*, 19 (2): 182–93.

Oxford Dictionary of English (2023), MobiSystems Incs.

Panskepp, J. (2004), *Affective Neuroscience: The Foundations of Human and Animal Emotions*. Oxford: Oxford University Press.

Parkes, N. A. (2018), 'The Power of Normal: Exploring the Notion of Story Structure', *World Literature Today*, 92 (3): 35–7.

Passmore, C., Gouvea, J. S. and R. Giere. (2014), 'Models in Science and in Learning Science: Focusing Scientific Practice on Sense-making', in M. Matthews (ed.), *International Handbook of Research in History, Philosophy and Science Teaching*, 1171–202, Dordrecht: Springer.

PBS NewsHour. (2019), *'The Power' Author Naomi Alderman Answers Your Questions*. Available at: https://www.pbs.org/newshour/show/the-power-author-naomi-alderman-answers-your-questions (Accessed: 4 December 2023).

Phillips, K. W., Liljenquist, K. A. and M. A. Neale (2009), 'Is the Pain Worth the Gain? The Advantages and Liabilities of Agreeing with Socially Distinct Newcomers', *Personality and Social Psychology Bulletin*, 35 (3): 336–50.

Piepenbring, D. (2015), 'Terry Pratchett, 1948–2015', *The Paris Review* (blog), 12 March. Available online: https://www.theparisreview.org/blog/2015/03/12/terry-pratchett-1948-2015/ (Accessed: 2 April 2023).

Pohl, C. and G. H. Hadorn (2008), 'Methodological Challenges of Transdisciplinary Research', *Natures Sciences Societies*, 16 (11): 111–21.

Popova, M. (2012), 'The Neurochemistry of Empathy, Storytelling, and the Dramatic Arc, Animated', *The Marginalian*, 3 October. Available online: https://www.themarginalian.org/2012/10/03/paul-zak-kirby-ferguson-storytelling/ (Accessed 15 December 2022).

Potgieter, F. and B. Smit (2009), 'Finding Academic Voice: A Critical Narrative of Knowledge-Making and Discovery', *Qualitative Inquiry*, 15: 214–28.

Priest, C. (2022), Interviewed by Joanne Anderton. 5 May, Email.

Qin, D. (2016), 'Positionality', in A. Wong, M. Wickramasinghe, R. Hoogland and N. A. Naples (eds), *The Wiley Blackwell Encyclopedia of Gender and Sexuality Studies*, 16 April. Available online: https://doi.org/10.1002/9781118663219.wbegss619 (Accessed: 14 March 2023).

Quesenberry, K. A. and M. K. Coolsen (2023), *Brand Storytelling: Integrated Marketing Communication for the Digital Media Landscape*, Lanham: Rowman & Littlefield.

Reina-Rozo, J. (2021), 'Art, Energy and Technology: The Solarpunk Movement', *International Journal of Engineering Social Justice and Peace*, 8: 55–68.

Repko, A. F. and R. Szostak (2011), *Interdisciplinary Research: Process and Theory*, Thousand Oaks: SAGE Publications.

Richmond, B. (1991), 'Systems Thinking: Four Key Questions', High Performance Systems, Inc. Available online: https://www.iseesystems.com/resources/articles/download/four-key-questions.pdf (Accessed: 14 March 2023).

Riggle, N. (2017), *On Being Awesome: A Unified Theory of How Not to Suck*, London: Penguin.

Ritchie, B. (2017), 'Writing into the Dark', *TEXT*, 21 (2), Available at: http://www.textjournal.com.au/oct17/ritchie.htm (Accessed: 1 July 2022).

Rittel, H. (1988), 'The Reasoning of Designers', in *Arbeitspapier A-88-4*. Stuttgart: Institut für Grundlagen der Planung, Universität Stuttgart.

Robinson, K. S. (1992), *Red Mars*, New York: Bantam Dell.

Robinson, K. S. (2002), *The Years of Rice and Salt*, New York: Bantam.

Robinson, K. S. (2020), *Ministry for the Future*, London: Orbit.

Robson, K. (2018), 'Another Word: Luke versus Han: An Approach to Characterization', *Clarkesworld Magazine*, Issue 136, January. Available online: https://clarkesworldmagazine.com/another_word_01_18/ (Accessed: 1 July 2022).

Rothman, J. (2019), 'How William Gibson Keeps His Science Fiction Real', *The New Yorker*, 9 December. Available online: https://www.newyorker.com/magazine/2019/12/16/how-william-gibson-keeps-his-science-fiction-real (Accessed: 2 April 2023).

Rutten, M. E. J., Dorée, A. G. and J. I. M. Halman (2013), 'Exploring the Value of a Novel Decision-making Theory in Understanding R&D Progress Decisions', *Management Decision*, 51 (1): 184–99.

Ryan, M. and N. K. Finney (2018), 'Science Fiction and the Strategist 2.0', *Strategy Bridge*, 27 August. Available online: https://thestrategybridge.org/the-bridge/2018/8/27/science-fiction-and-the-strategist-20 (Accessed: 4 December 2023).

Ryan, M. (2020), 'The Intellectual Edge: A Competitive Advantage for Future War and Strategic Competition', *Joint Force Quarterly*, 96 (1st Quarter): 6–11.

Ryan, M.-L. (1980), 'Fiction, Non-factuals, and the Principle of Minimal Departure', *Poetics*, 9: 403–22.

Ryan, M.-L. (2015), 'Transmedia Storytelling: Industry Buzzword or New Narrative Experience?', *Storyworlds: A Journal of Narrative Studies*, 7 (2): 1–19.

Ryan, M. (2019), *An Australian Intellectual Edge for Conflict and Competition in the 21st Century*, Canberra: Strategic & Defence Studies Centre.

Ryan, M.-L. and J.-N. Thon (2014), 'Storyworlds Across Media: Introduction', in M.-L. Ryan and J.-N. Thon (eds), *Storyworlds Across Media: Toward a Media-Conscious Narratology*, 1–24, Lincoln and London: University of Nebraska Press.

Saler, M. (2012), *As If: Modern Enchantment and the Literary Pre-History of Virtual Reality*, Oxford, New York: Oxford University Press.

Samuelson, D. N. (1993), 'Modes of Extrapolation: The Formulas of Hard SF', *Science Fiction Studies*, 20 (2): 191–232.

Samutina, N. (2016), 'Fan Fiction as World-building: Transformative Reception in Crossover Writing', *Continuum: Journal of Media & Cultural Studies*, 30 (4): 433–50.

Schleicher, D., Jones, P. and O. Kachur (2010), 'Bodystorming as Embodied Designing', *Interactions*, 17: 47–51.

Schmidt, L., Falk, T., Siegmund-Schultze, M. and J. H. Spangenberg (2020), 'The Objectives of Stakeholder Involvement in Transdisciplinary Research: A Conceptual Framework for a Reflective and Reflexive Practise', *Ecological Economics*, 176 (106751): 1–9.

Schwarz, J. O. (2008), 'Assessing the Future of Futures Studies in Management', *Futures*, 40 (3): 237–46.

Scoblic, J. P. (2020), 'Strategic Foresight as Dynamic Capability: A New Lens on Knightian Uncertainty', *Harvard Business School Working Paper No. 20-093*. Available online: www.hbs.edu/faculty/Pages/item.aspx?num=57819 (Accessed: 4 December 2023).

Scullard, L. (2012), 'Worldbuilding in SF – Advice Taken from the Great Terry Pratchett', *Lisa Scullard*, 1 May. Available online: https://lisascullard.wordpress.com/2012/05/01/worldbuilding-in-sf-advice-taken-from-the-great-terry-pratchett/ (Accessed: 16 February 2023).

Segura, E. M., Spiel, K., Johansson, K., Back, J., Toups Dugas, P. O., Hammer, J., Waern, A., Tanenbaum, T. J. and K. Isbister (2019), 'Larping (Live Action Role Playing) as an Embodied Design Research Method', *DIS '19 Companion: Companion Publication of the 2019 on Designing Interactive Systems Conference*: 389–92.

Shankar, P. R. (2009), 'Creative Writing and Medical Education', *Journal of Clinical and Diagnostic Research*, 3 (3): 1603–7.

Shawl, N. (2009), 'Transracial Writing for the Sincere', *Science Fiction & Fantasy Writers Association*, 4 December. Available online: https://www.sfwa.org/2009/12/04/transracial-writing-for-the-sincere/ (Accessed: 14 February 2023).

Shawl, N. and C. Ward (2005), *Writing the Other: A Practical Approach*. Seattle: Aqueduct Press.

Shklovskij, V. (1998), 'Art as Technique', in J. Rivkin and M. Ryan (eds), *Literary Theory: An Anthology*, Malden: Blackwell Publishing, 8–14.

Sicart, M. (2014), *Play Matters*, Cambridge, MA: MIT Press.

Silva, T. C. and P. de Tarso Fonseca Silva (2022), *Making Sense of Work Through Collaborative Storytelling: Building Narratives in Organisational Change*, Cham: Palgrave Macmillan.

The Simpsons (2000), [TV Programme] 'Bart to the Future', Season 11 (17), Fox, 19 March.

Sisterson, C., Spain, J. and L. Nugent (2021), 'The Great Debate: Plotting vs Pantsing', *Good Reading*, May: 16–17.

Spenser, E. (1978), *The Faerie Queene*, eds T. P. Roche Jr and C. P. O'Donnell Jr, London: Penguin.

Stackelberg, P. and A. McDowell (2015), 'What in the World? Storyworlds, Science Fiction, and Futures Studies', *Journal of Futures Studies*, 20 (2): 25–46.

Stark, L. (2014), 'A Primer on Safety in Roleplaying Games', *Leaving Mundania: Inside the World of Larp*, 27 February. Available online: https://leavingmundania.com/2014/02/27/primer-safety-in-roleplaying-games/ (Accessed: 2 November 2023).

Stevenson, T. (2001), 'The Futures of Futures Studies', *Futures*, 33: 665–9.

Storr, W. (2020), *The Science of Storytelling: Why Stories Make Us Human and How to Tell Them Better*, New York: Abrams Press.

Sullivan, G. 2010, *Art Practice as Research: Inquiry in Visual Arts*, 2nd edn, Thousand Oaks: SAGE.

Suvin, D. ([1979] 2016), *Metamorphoses of Science Fiction: On the Poetics and History of a Literary Genre*, Oxford: Peter Lang.

Sword, H. (2012), *Stylish Academic Writing*. Cambridge, MA: Harvard University Press.

Taleb, N. N. (2007), *The Black Swan: The Impact of the Highly Improbable*, New York: Random House.

Thornton, M. A. and D. I. Tamir (2021), 'People Accurately Predict the Transition Probabilities between Actions', *Science Advances*, 7 (9): 1–11.

Tidhar, L. (2022), Interviewed by Lisa Bennett. 5 May, Zoom.

Tiptree Jr, J. (1986), 'The Only Neat Thing to Do', in *The Starry Rift*, Kindle edn, New York: Tor.

Toffler, A. (1970), *Future Shock*, New York: Random House.

Tolkien, J. R. R. ([1945] 2008), *On Fairy-Stories*, eds V. Flieger and D. A. Anderson, New York: HarperCollins.

Tolkien, J. R. R. (2013), *The Hobbit*. London: HarperCollins.

Tsukawaki, R., Imura, T., Kojima, N., Furukawa, Y. and K. Ito (2020), 'The Correlation between Teachers' Humor and Class Climate: A Study Targeting Primary and Secondary School Students', *HUMOR*, 33 (3): 405–21.

Ulnicane, I. (2015) 'Why Do International Research Collaborations Last?', *Science and Public Policy*, 42 (4): 433–47.

VanderMeer, J. (2013), *Wonderbook: The Illustrated Guide to Creating Imaginative Fiction*, New York: Abrams Image.

Vanderslice, S. (2010), 'Once More to the Workshop: A Myth Caught in Time', in D. Donnelly (ed.), *Does the Writing Workshop Still Work?*, 30–5, Bristol; Blue Ridge Summit: Multilingual Matters.

Varotsi, L. (2019), *Conceptualisation and Exposition: A Theory of Character Construction*, Milton: Taylor & Francis Group.

Vertisi, J. (2019), '"All These Worlds are Yours Except … "': Science Fiction and Folk Fictions at NASA', *Engaging Science, Technology and Society*, 5: 135–59.

Victoria-Uribe, R. and M. E. González-Alcaraz (2021), 'No Elf is an Island: Understanding Worldbuilding through System Thinking', in F. T. Barbini (ed.), *Worlds Apart: Worldbuilding in Fantasy and Science Fiction*, 8–17, La Vergne: Luna Press Publishing.

Vint, S. (2021), *Science Fiction*, Cambridge, MA: The MIT Press.

Voigts-Virchow, E. (2012), 'Pride and Promiscuity and Zombies, or: Miss Austen Mashed Up in the Affinity Spaces of Participatory Culture', in P. Nicklas and O. Lindner (eds), *Adaptation and Cultural Appropriation: Literature, Film, and the Arts*, 34–56, Berlin; Boston: De Gruyter.

Vonnegut, K. (2005). *A Man Without a Country*, New York: Seven Stories Press.

von Thienen, J. P. A., Clancey, W. J., Corazza, G. E. and C. Meinel (2018), 'Theoretical Foundations of Design Thinking', in H. Plattner, C. Meinel and L. Leifer (eds), *Design Thinking Research: Understanding Innovation*, 13–40, Cham: Springer.

Wack, P. (1985), 'Scenarios: Shooting the Rapids', *Harvard Business Review*, 63 (6): 139–50.

Walton, J. L. and P. Levontin (eds), *Vector*, 297 (Spring 2023), The British Science Fiction Association.

Ward, J. and H. Shortt (2020), 'Using Arts-Based Methods of Research: A Critical Introduction to the Development of Arts-Based Research Methods', in J. Ward and H. Shortt (eds), *Using Arts-Based Research Methods: Creative Approaches for Researching Business, Organisation and Humanities*, 1–13, London: Palgrave Macmillan.

Warzel, D. (2011), 'Wikihistory', *Tor.com*, 31 August. Available online: https://www.tor.com/2011/08/31/wikihistory/ (Accessed: 4 December 2023).

Weir, A. (2014), *The Martian*, New York: Random House.

White, B. Y. (1993), 'ThinkerTools: Causal Models, Conceptual Change, and Science Education', *Cognition and Instruction*, 10 (1): 1–100.

White, G. (2013), 'Introduction', in *Audience Participation in Theatre*, 1–28, London: Palgrave Macmillan.

Whitehead, N. P., Scherer, W. T. and M. C. Smith (2014), 'Systems Thinking About Systems Thinking a Proposal for a Common Language', *IEEE Systems Journal*, 9 (40): 1117–28.

Whitehouse, M., Rahm, H., Wozniak, S., Breunig, S., De Nardi, G., Dionne, F., Fujio, M., Graf, E-M., Matic, I., McKenna, C. J., Steiner, F. and S. Svik̦e (2021) 'Developing Shared Languages: The Fundamentals of Mutual Learning and Problem Solving in Transdisciplinary Collaboration', *AILA Review*, 34 (1): 1–18.

Whittle, J. (2014), 'How Much Participation Is Enough? A Comparison of Six Participatory Design Projects in Terms of Outcomes', in *Proceedings of the 13th Participatory Design Conference: Research Papers – Volume 1*, 121–30, New York: Association for Computing Machinery.

Wilkins, K. (2012), 'Genre and Speculative Fiction', in D. Morley and P. Neilsen (eds), *The Cambridge Companion to Creative Writing*, 37–51, Cambridge: Cambridge University Press.

Wilkins, K. (2019), *Young Adult Fantasy Fiction: Conventions, Originality, Reproducibility*, Cambridge: Cambridge University Press.

Wilkins, K. (2024), 'Three New Myths for Inspiration', in M. Moore and S. Meekings (eds), *The Scholarship of Creative Writing Practice: Beyond Craft, Pedagogy, and the Academy*, 9–22, London: Bloomsbury.

Wilkins, K., Bennett, H. and H. Marshall (2023), 'Calibrating Possibility', *Possibility Studies and Society*, 1 (1–2): 1–6. Available online: https://journals.sagepub.com/doi/10.1177/27538699231166486 (Accessed: 4 December 2023).

Wilkins, K., Driscoll, B. and L. Fletcher (2022), *Genre Worlds: Popular Fiction and 21st-Century Book Culture*, Amherst: University of Massachusetts Press.

Williams, R. ([1958] 1989), *Resources of Hope*, London: Verso.

Wilson, M. (2018), 'Patriarchs on Pedestals? How Doctors are Taught to Improve their Bedside Manner', *The Conversation*, 19 June. Available online: https://theconversation.com/patriarchs-on-pedestals-how-doctors-are-taught-to-improve-their-bedside-manner-95863 (Accessed: 12 October 2023).

Wolf, M. J. P. (2012), *Building Imaginary Worlds: The Theory and History of Subcreation*, New York: Routledge.

Wood, J. (2008), *How Fiction Works*, London: Jonathan Cape.

Yanai, I. and M. Lercher (2019), 'Night Science', *Genome Biology*, 20 (179): 1–3.

Zaidi, L. (2018), Building Brave New Worlds: Science Fiction and Transition Design. [Master of Design, Strategic Foresight and Innovation, Ontario College of Art and Design]. Available online: http://dx.doi.org/10.2139/ssrn.3217423 (Accessed: 2 January 2022).

Zaidi, L. (2019), 'Worldbuilding in Science Fiction, Foresight, and Design', *Journal of Futures Studies*, 23 (4): 15–26.

INDEX